D0938632

GREECE BEFORE HISTORY

GREECE
BEFORE HISTORY

AN ARCHAEOLOGICAL
COMPANION AND GUIDE

Curtis Runnels • Priscilla Murray

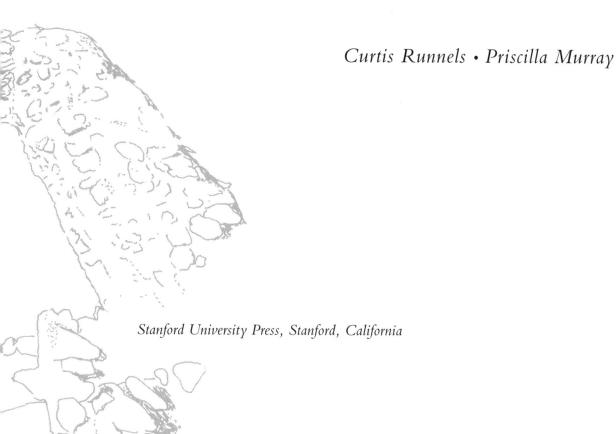

Stanford University Press, Stanford, California

Stanford University Press
Stanford, California
© 2001 by the Board of Trustees of the
Leland Stanford Junior University

Printed in the United States of America
on acid-free, archival-quality paper

Library of Congress Cataloging-in-Publication Data

Runnels, Curtis Neil
    Greece before history : an archaeological companion
  and guide / Curtis Runnels, Priscilla Murray.
      p. cm.
    Includes bibliographical references and index.
    ISBN 0-8047-4036-4 (alk. paper) —
    ISBN 0-8047-4050-X (pbk.: alk. paper)
     I. Prehistoric peoples—Greece.   2. Antiquities,
  Prehistoric—Greece.   I. Murray, Priscilla.   II. Title.
  GN815.R85   2001
  937.6—dc21   00-058835

Designed by Eleanor Mennick
Typeset by G&S Typesetters in 11/14 Monotype Bembo

Original Printing 2001
Last figure below indicates year of this printing:
10 09 08 07 06 05 04 03 02 01

 *Contents*

List of Illustrations

This book belongs to the genre of scientific writing called "popular," in that it is intended to present scientific findings to a general readership. By "general readership," we mean anyone with a curiosity about archaeology in general, and the archaeology of Greece in particular. We have drawn upon our own familiarity with the vast technical, and usually off-putting, literature on the subject, and on our own original research and experience in fieldwork to obtain the material for this book. Although the summary of what archaeology can tell us about Greek prehistory is based on solid evidence and scientific fact, we have spiced the text with touches of humor and personal reflection and illustrated it with drawings chosen for their visual appeal. It is our firm belief that there is a need for this sort of book.

Periodic "stock-taking" of what is, and is not, known about the archaeology of a particular period or place is useful for students, travelers, and all those who are interested in the subject but do not have the time to examine and digest the large amount of information in excavation reports and specialized scientific journals. The writing of this book has been useful for us as well by giving us the opportunity and incentive to take a broad look at the knowledge gained by archaeology in the past 25 years. We hope that this attempt to present the "big picture" intrigues and satisfies our readers. And we hope that our professional colleagues will have sympathy with our motives and forgive us our omissions and mistakes.

Books are made from trees, but they do not grow on them. They take shape over time as the result of inspiration, research, analysis, study, and much hard work, all of which require authors to rely for advice and help on individuals and institutions too numerous to mention. Because of the length of time required to bring this book into existence, we owe an especially large debt of this kind. We have been working on the idea for this book in one form or another for more than ten years. The writing of the text alone took two years, mostly in the form of one- or two-week periods of work squeezed into the ever smaller spaces in our professional schedules of administration, teaching, and fieldwork. The experience and research that make this book possible span a period of more than 25 years.

The structure and content of the book took shape as we read the literature, talked with students, friends, and colleagues from around the world while visiting archaeological sites, and carried out our own fieldwork. Here then is our digested, synthesized, and abstracted view of the present state of prehistoric archaeology in Greece. To tease apart the whole and identify every influence, cite every source, or name every individual who has contributed in some way to this work is beyond our power. We would certainly fail to identify them all, but we are truly grateful to all those who, although not acknowledged individually, have contributed to our thinking about Greek prehistory.

We owe a special debt to the institutions that made this work possible over the years, especially the Society of Antiquaries of London and the National Geographic Society, which supported our work with grants. The Institute for Aegean Prehistory (INSTAP) provided the lion's share of funding for our research since 1984; this one institution has done more than any other foundation to promote research in this area. The support of INSTAP has grown more important in the past decade as other sources of funding for Greek archaeology have disappeared. The founder of INSTAP, Malcolm Wiener, deserves our special gratitude and respect for his vision and generosity, and it is a special pleasure to acknowledge him here. We wish also to thank the American School of Classical Studies at Athens, which was our base of operations while working in Greece, and Eliza McClennen, who prepared the maps. Karl Petruso, best friend and colleague, kindly read the manuscript in great detail in an early draft and made many useful suggestions, both large and small, which were always helpful. Norris Pope, the director of Stanford University Press, deserves our thanks for his support of this project from its inception.

Traditional age	Period	Culture name	Calendar date
Bronze	Late	Minoan/Mycenaean	1600–1100 B.C.
	Middle	Minoan	2100–1600 B.C.
	Early	Minoan	3600–2100 B.C.
		Cycladic	
		Helladic	
Neolithic	Final		4500–3600 B.C.
	Late		5500–4500 B.C.
	Middle		6000–5500 B.C.
	Early		6850–6000 B.C.
Mesolithic	Upper		10,500–9000 B.C.
	Lower		
Palaeolithic	Upper	Aurignacian	30,000–13,000 B.P.
	Middle	Mousterian	150,000–30,000 B.P.
	Lower	Acheulean	400,000–150,000 B.P.

NOTES: All dates are approximate and are given as B.P. (before present, i.e., 1950) or B.C. (before the common era). See Appendix A for a discussion of these dates. The Palaeolithic, Mesolithic, and Neolithic are subdivisions of the Stone Age. The names of the periods reflect the different backgrounds of the archaeologists who did the naming. The Early Stone Age names show the influence of geology, and the Neolithic and Bronze Age names derive from humanistic classifications. There are inconsistencies in the culture names. The culture names should end in "-an" and derive from a type site (note that Cycladic and Helladic are the outliers) and for some reason there are no agreed-upon culture names for the Mesolithic and Neolithic periods. Note, too, that the terms "Cycladic" and "Minoan" are also used for the Middle and Late Bronze Age; "Late Helladic" can substitute for "Mycenaean."

GREECE BEFORE HISTORY

CHAPTER ONE

AN INTRODUCTION TO THE PREHISTORY OF GREECE

There are many books about the archaeology of Greece that provide historical and literary background information, along with detailed descriptions of archaeological sites and museums accompanied by plans and illustrations of artifacts. Some are written for the student or general reader; others are aimed at travelers and supply information on restaurants, hotels, and local customs. As contemporary readers have developed more specialized tastes and interests, new books have addressed these trends. Many readers go to Greece only in their dreams, and they read books on archaeology and travel in order to satisfy their curiosity; others prefer to do their reading after they have visited the country in order to gain additional insights or refresh their memories. And others, perhaps the majority, wish a book to serve as a useful companion in their travels, one that will be on hand to answer questions that arise during visits to archaeological sites and museums. Perhaps ambitiously, we hope to satisfy all of these readers with this book. It is intended as a guide and a companion for all visitors, whether they travel to Greece on an airplane or a ship, in a classroom, or in a favorite reading chair.

In reviewing the books on Greek archaeology written over the past 25 years we found that most of them concentrate on the classical Greco-Roman past, and to a lesser extent on Byzantine Greece. Far fewer attempt to interest readers in the long, rich, prehistoric past of Greece, a country with one of the oldest archaeological records of all the European nations.

The first human beings to leave Africa and migrate to Europe passed through Greece. It was on the fertile plains of central and northern Greece that early farmers established their villages and created the first civilization on European soil. Later still, the legendary civilizations of Minoan Crete and Mycenae were established in southern Greece and the islands of the Aegean Sea. These civilizations made many important contributions to later Western civilization, particularly in the area of myth and legend. In our own day, poets, artists, writers, and even Hollywood producers tell the stories of gods, kings, and heroes from the Mycenaean and Minoan world: Agamemnon, Achilles, Odysseus, and Helen belong to the great cycle of the Trojan War. Minos, the Labyrinth, the Minotaur, the great hero Theseus, and the great legends that surround them are woven into the tapestry of our entire culture. Even the mysteriously popular legend of Atlantis has its roots firmly grounded in the deep prehistory of the Greek world.

Books devoted to Greek prehistory for the general reader and traveler are exceedingly rare. There are notable exceptions, particularly the well-written but sadly out-of-date work by Emily Vermeule, *Greece in the Bronze Age*, and some short guides to specific prehistoric sites, such as George Mylonas's *Mycenae: A Guide*. We hope to fill this gap in the literature and have written this book for students, travelers, and the simply curious who wish to know something about Greece before history. We often meet people who want to know about the oddly shaped mounds ("tells" to an archaeologist) that dot the countryside; about the uses of the curious Stone Age flints seen in museum cases; or about the brightly colored pots and mysterious anthropomorphic figurines from prehistoric times in museums around the world. This book is also for those who want to know more about the foundations of later, historical, Greece. Finally, this book is for students of all ages and levels who simply want to know more about the marvelous accomplishments of Europe's first great civilization.

The approach we take in this book is not one widely used in scientific writing, even for general audiences. The chronological outlines of prehistoric cultures, as well as descriptions of artifacts, architecture, burial customs, and the like, will be familiar. But our more personal observations and attempts to interpret these facts are not "objective" in the usual scientific sense. Although we make every effort to ground our interpretations on the available evidence, we occasionally go beyond the strict limits of the evidence to offer our own views on the past, which are sometimes based as much on intuition and experience as on logical deduction from theory. Some of our conclusions are the result of long reflection on a group of related problems; sometimes these conclusions are hard to put into words, and even harder to justify with the scattered bits of evidence that we have in hand. Given the lack of books on this subject, we believe this approach is justified, even necessary. We hope to stimulate dialogue by inviting readers to consider the evidence and reach their own conclusions.

Part of the novelty of this book resides in its dual use, as indicated by the subtitle: "An Archaeological Companion and Guide." In this guide we present our evidence and conclusions in an orderly manner on the page, which allows all readers access; but we also want this to be a guide in the sense of a traveler's "companion." We know the frustrating experience of the traveler with limited time who finds himself or herself standing before a museum case crowded with artifacts but no labels, or looking out over a jumble of ruins with no means of distinguishing what is important from what is mere rubbish. Because we have sympathy for serious travelers and tourists, we have included a chapter (Chapter 7) and an appendix (Appendix C) that will help to make sense of what they see in Greece. For readers and travelers alike, the drawings herein have been carefully selected to provide a visual inventory of the scenery, typical artifacts, and the most important monuments and sites that the traveler will encounter. For example, Figure 1.1 shows the typical vegetation, architecture, and terrain of a seaside village. Thus this guide is both a reference for home or classroom use and a traveler's *vade mecum*.

Now let us go on an imaginary journey into the prehistoric past of Greece. Traveling back in time, we quickly pass through the Ottoman

1.1   The Greek countryside.

and Byzantine periods with their light-filled mosques and churches encrusted with frescoes and smoking with incense (see Figure 1.2). Further back in time we encounter the Greco-Roman world of classical antiquity with its marble-strewn cities and temple precincts sprouting forests of columns. Processions of people wind their way up to the Parthenon, and the dark gray-blue Aegean is filled with the sails of ships.

We soon leave these behind us, for the historical record is not very deep—a mere two and a half millennia. And we travel on, finding before us a broad vista of prehistoric cultures, still only imperfectly known from archaeological research. In the foreground is the barbarous splendor of the tombs and palaces of the Minoan and later Mycenaean civilizations and farther away a long stretch of earlier Bronze Age civilizations with bronze weapons, long oared ships, and startling, yet diminutive, marble sculptures of men and gods. And even more distant on the horizon we see the sunlit villages of the first farmers in Europe, pioneers from Asia Minor who colonized Greece more than 9,000 years ago in one of the greatest adventures of humankind's early history.

Smoke rises from brightly painted adobe brick houses, and in the fields harvesters wield stone knives. As we come closer, we see others

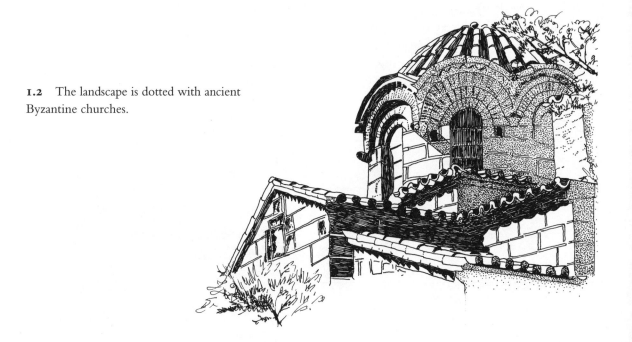

1.2   The landscape is dotted with ancient Byzantine churches.

working in the open spaces of the village, fashioning figures of humans in clay and stone and painting pots with brilliant patterns of red and black. Although simple, these villages with their agriculture and industrial arts are still familiar. At the end of our journey, at the edge of our vision, we begin to see the very different people of the Old Stone Age. Villages of clay give way to caves and tented campsites, and instead of farmers we see small groups of people hunting wild oxen, bison, elephant, and rhinoceros on windswept, treeless plains. In a landscape where people are strangely rare, small groups at the farthest edges gather nuts and fruits along the banks of streams and lakes. This dreamlike, even fantastic, picture has no certain limits: it extends as far as we can see.

At the extreme limit of our vision we perceive the oldest inhabitants of the land we know as Greece; shadowy figures who are not fully human, but something other. When we consider that the earliest inhabitants of this land may have lived more than 400,000 years ago, the 2,000 or 3,000 years allotted to all of the recorded history of Greece seems like thin, light-catching froth on the surface of a deep ocean of human existence. This book is about the long record of prehistoric Greece, the record of human actions and achievements before the beginning of recorded history.

FIRST THINGS

Let us begin by clarifying what we mean by "prehistoric." Technically, prehistoric means "before history," which begins when populations began keeping written records of the names of individual people and some account of the actions and events that took place in the past. Prehistoric cultures, by definition, are not known from such records; they are eternally anonymous and silent, known only from the work of archaeologists who have excavated buildings and burials, classified tools and weapons, and described and catalogued pottery, jewelry, and idols of now nameless and forgotten gods.

According to long-standing and ancient tradition, Greek history begins with the first Olympic games in 776 B.C. The rich accounts of ancient, medieval, and modern Greek history after this time are themselves the invention of the Greeks, who created the discipline of historical writing. All historians of the West trace their discipline back to, among others, Herodotus, Thucydides, and Xenophon, the first historians known to the world. With such a tradition, not surprisingly, scholars have paid less attention to the long record of human achievement that took place before history began.

The greatest of the ancient historians, Thucydides (ca. 460–400 B.C.), began his account of the Peloponnesian War with twelve chapters in a book that outlined the social and political conditions of Greece before his own time. He traced the peopling of Greece from the first migrating bands to the founding of walled towns, and to the first great event in the history of Greece: the Trojan War. As interesting and perceptive as it is, the "archaeology" of Thucydides was entirely speculative. Although Thucydides uses ethnographic "evidence" to describe the arms of the "barbarians" (that is, non-Greek peoples) and the fashions of Greek tribes, he uses archaeological evidence only once. In his account of the Athenian ritual of purification of the Cycladic island of Delos, Thucydides cites the non-Greek nature of the funerary remains that were removed from the island after burial was prohibited there. The weapons and the method of burial were regarded as evidence that the earlier inhabitants of the Cycladic islands were Carians from Asia Minor. Otherwise his "evidence" seems to be based almost exclusively on careful study of Homer and oral traditions. The interest of these chapters lies mainly in his sober, rational, and believable reconstruction of early Greek life that does not appeal to the mythical or the fantastic for explanation. But it is merely an imaginary narrative, however credible, composed by lamplight and unsupported by scientific evidence.

Thucydides is nevertheless an important guide and mentor for the prehistorian as well as the historian. In addition to providing sober, careful analysis, he contributed the vital insight that human nature is constant, and he believed that a thorough analysis of the wars and events that gripped his own time would help future historians understand the events of their own eras. "It will be enough for me," he tells us, "if these words of mine are judged useful by those who want to understand clearly the events which happened in the past and which (human nature being what it is) will, at some time or other and in much the same ways, be repeated in the future." Although his assessment of human nature was essentially negative ("human nature, always ready to offend even where laws exist, showed itself proudly in its true colours, as something incapable of controlling passion"), Thucydides nevertheless underscores the value of the assumption of a constant nature for historians. Astronomers have found that they must assume that the laws of nature in distant galaxies are the same as the laws of our own solar system if they are to infer anything about what they cannot see; the same is true for paleontologists and archaeologists. The same constancy of human nature assumed by Thucydides allows us to judge and interpret the actions and even the motives of long-dead peoples in distant and extinct cultures. Without this assumption, archaeological inference would be impossible.

On the basis of a century of prehistoric archaeological research, prehistorians of Greece have divided the hundreds of thousands of years of prehistoric life into carefully defined periods with technical names—the Palaeolithic and Mesolithic periods (together, the Old Stone Age in popular writing), the Neolithic period (the New Stone Age), the Bronze Age, and the Iron Age, which was initially prehistoric (the Early Iron Age) but in the end encompasses all of the historic cultures of classical antiquity. This classification system was invented by nineteenth-century European antiquarians in Denmark and Sweden and goes back, by way of the Roman poet and philosopher Lucretius, to the ancient Greek philosophers, in particular the Boeotian poet Hesiod, one of the first to order the human past in a series of "ages." The three-age system is somewhat too simple and general for use in contemporary scientific archaeology, but it is useful for conceiving of the enormous scope of the human past. In this book, we are concerned with the first two ages, the Stone Age, which comprises the Palaeolithic, Mesolithic, and Neolithic subdivisions, and the Bronze Age, a much shorter period known chiefly for the glamorous Minoan and Mycenaean civilizations.

THE PLAN OF THIS WORK

This book organizes archaeological information by period, starting with the Palaeolithic, continuing through the Neolithic, and concluding with the end of the Bronze Age. Each period is illustrated with line drawings of typical artifacts and architecture rather than photographs, which usually accompany books written for the general reader. This rather old-fashioned approach perhaps requires some explanation. Line drawings are commonly used by archaeologists to communicate their findings to each other, and drawings, though less precise than photographs, can capture the essential features of a site or artifact, highlighting what the archaeologist thinks is important about them. Not incidentally, they are an attractive visual accompaniment to the text while at the same time helping the reader to recognize the essential characteristics of the material culture of prehistoric Greece. We have tried to include artifacts and views that are not commonly found in other publications.

Another feature of this book that is not found in the usual archaeological treatise is some practical information for travelers, whether students or seasoned professionals. Chapter 7 and Appendix C contain additional suggestions for an archaeological tour.

We have dispensed with footnotes in order to allow the text to flow freely, without interruption. The Bibliographic Essay at the end guides the reader to the sources of facts and theories mentioned in the text and suggests further reading.

Finally, let us say a word about ourselves. Because this is such a highly personal narrative and interpretation, it is only fair for the reader to know who we are and where we stand. We are professional archaeologists, both trained in the fields of archaeology and anthropology, with a life-long interest in prehistoric cultures of Europe and the Mediterranean world. We first met on a prehistoric excavation in southern Greece in the early 1970s and have traveled and worked together on archaeological projects in Greece and Turkey ever since. In recent years we have been particularly interested in understanding the Palaeolithic cultures of this region, which have been much neglected, partly because they have been overshadowed by the illustrious civilizations of classical antiquity and partly because of the fragmentary nature of the evidence. This curiosity has led us to explore much of Greece, and on the way we have developed our own personal, and perhaps idiosyncratic, view of Greek prehistory. Our decades of joint research have brought us to the point where we wish to share our views with people other than specialists.

This book is the result of many years of private discussions across tables stacked high with artifacts and during long, usually hot, days of fieldwork, sometimes over the dinner table in the lingering twilight of evening, and, more often than not, during long walks in the unforgettable mountain country of Greece in its springtime glory. Now we are ready to invite the reader to join in our conversation.

CHAPTER TWO

THE OLD STONE AGE

How It All Began

Long before there was a "Greece," and long before history, there was the land. Along the rocky, dusty trails, across icy mountain passes, and over the swampy lowlands the primitive ancestors of our human race migrated from the primeval homeland in search of better climates, food, and the other necessities of life as they knew it. The land we today call the Balkans (Ottoman Turkish for "wooded mountains"), of which Greece is the lonely southern tip, forms a natural bridge connecting Asia with Europe (see Figure 2.1). This bridge has been crossed and recrossed, not only by our early ancestors, but countless times by migrants, explorers, and conquerors. Here we are concerned with the first early humans (technically, hominids) to make the journey. Where they started is relatively well understood, but everything else, including the exact timing of their arrival, their precise route, and even their relationship to our own species, is shrouded in uncertainty.

Let us begin with their homeland. The best current scientific information indicates that the ancestors of all humans alive today made their appearance in Africa some 4 to 5 million years ago. The first recognizable human ancestor (hominid) appeared in the geological epoch known as the Pliocene (which began 5 1/2 million years ago) and is known as *Australopithecus afarensis*. The physical evolution of human beings unfolded against a background of changing climates on a global scale, particularly as the Pliocene gave way to the Pleistocene epoch

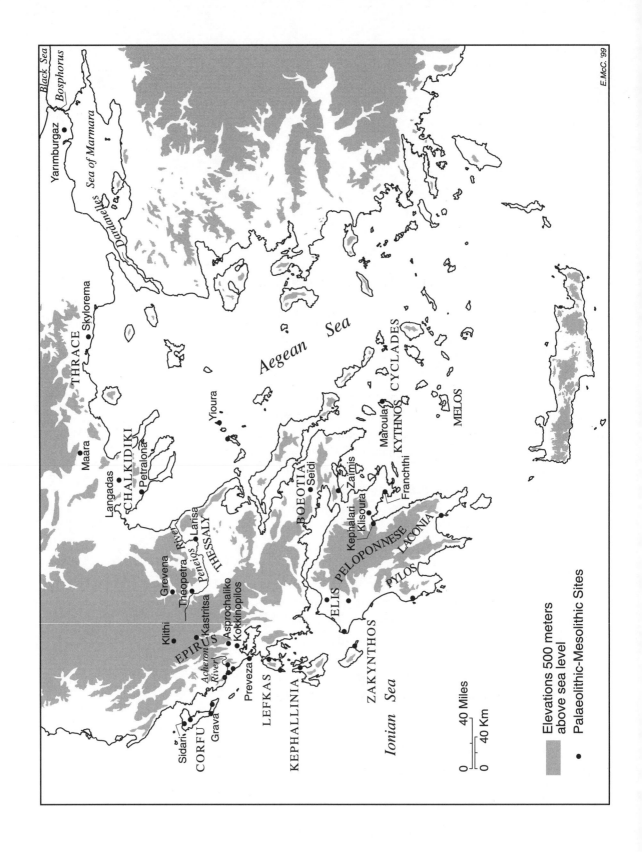

Black Sea

Bosphorus

Yarımburgaz

Sea of Marmara

Dardanelles

THRACE

Skylorema

Aegean Sea

Maara

Langadas

CHALKIDIKI

Petralona

Vioura

Larisa

Peneios River

THESSALY

Grevena

Theopetra River

Klithi

Kastritsa

Asprochaliko

EPIRUS

Acheron River

Kokkinopilos

Preveza

LEFKAS

Sidari

CORFU

Grava

KEPHALLINIA

ZAKYNTHOS

Ionian Sea

BOEOTIA

Seidi

Zaimis

Kephalari

Klisoura

Franchthi

Maroula

KYTHNOS

CYCLADES

MELOS

PELOPONNESE

ELIS

LACONIA

PYLOS

Elevations 500 meters
above sea level

Palaeolithic-Mesolithic Sites

40 Miles

40 Km

E.McC. '99

(about 1.8 million years ago). At that time the world entered the most recent of several great Ice Ages: the ice caps expanded and global temperatures fell sharply.

The oldest fossil evidence for primitive species of human precursors has been found in abundance in the Great Rift Valley of East Africa from Ethiopia south to Kenya and Tanzania, as well as in South Africa and farther to the west in Uganda, Algeria, and Morocco. The earliest hominid species, *Australopithecus afarensis*, was long-lived, persisting for as long as a million years, but was eventually replaced or succeeded by one or more similar species. We are interested only in the lineage that led to our own species. This lineage appears to be descended from the hominids *Australopithecus africanus* and *Homo habilis*, which lived in east Africa between 3 and 1 1/2 million years ago, overlapping the transition from the Pliocene to the Pleistocene. All of the early hominids exhibit some uniquely human characteristics, including upright bipedal posture, large brains, small faces, hands with opposable thumbs, and a dependence on stone tools and other implements for gaining subsistence.

It would be unproductive to concern ourselves overmuch with the details of human evolution. Briefly, however, the different species of early humans are known by a variety of scientific names—*Homo habilis*, *Homo erectus* (a.k.a. *Homo ergaster*), and *Homo rudolfensis*. Specialists are divided over the relationships among these fossil hominids and are uncertain how to relate them to modern humans (*Homo sapiens sapiens*). Some specialists, jocularly referred to as "lumpers," believe that there was probably only one species in existence at any one time, or at most two, and that the different fossil forms are only variant forms of one species. The lumpers hold that because early hominids appear to have varied in their physical form they can be grouped together on the basis of shared characteristics. Another group of specialists, however, called "splitters," use the same variability of form in the fossil specimens to divide hominids into numerous separate species. There is no way to be certain which view is correct because only a few hundred hominid fossils have been found in Africa

2.1 *Opposite.* The locations of the principal known Palaeolithic and Mesolithic sites. They are found in almost all regions but are rare in the smaller Cycladic islands and the mountainous interior of the mainland. There are no sites of this period on Crete.

since 1925 (when fossil hunting began), the difference in their age spans a period of as long as 4 million years, and they have been found hundreds and even thousands of kilometers apart.

In the absence of definite evidence one way or the other, physical anthropologists can only speculate about the relationships between any two specimens, and it is probable that the growing number of expeditions and the larger samples of well-dated specimens they are recovering will only serve to make the picture more complicated. For our purposes, we do not need to be overly concerned about the lack of certainty. Of the early forms of fossil hominids, the only ones found outside Africa have been *Homo erectus* (or *Homo ergaster* in the Near East and Asia), the recently identified *Homo antecessor* (in Spain), and the hominid known as *Homo heidelbergensis* in Europe. In Greece the earliest fossil hominids belong to this group of advanced hominids (*Homo heidelbergensis*) from the period after humans had already evolved toward *Homo sapiens*. One thing is clear, however: the decisive steps in the evolution of humanity took place in Africa long before humans migrated to Greece.

The geological period known as the Pleistocene is the epoch that precedes our own, the Holocene, which began a mere 10,000 years ago, but archaeologists have decided to confuse the general public by creating their own system of classifying the human past. The archaeological period that coincides more or less with the Pleistocene is known as the Stone Age, which extends from 2.5 million years to barely 5,000 years ago. For convenience, the period has been divided into three stages, the Palaeolithic (Old Stone Age), the Mesolithic (technically the Middle Stone Age, but usually lumped with the Old Stone Age), and the Neolithic (New Stone Age) (see Figure 2.2).

THE PALAEOLITHIC PERIOD

The Palaeolithic is the longest stage of the Stone Age. The distinguishing feature of the Palaeolithic is the economy of early humans: they were hunters of wild animals and gatherers of wild plants, foragers moving in small bands of 20–50 closely related persons with a technology limited to tools and weapons of wood, skin, bone, and stone. Owing to the vagaries of organic preservation, only stone tools typically survive; hence the general appellation "Stone Age." Variations in the types of stone tools found in archaeological sites allow the Palaeolithic to be subdivided into separate phases.

In the earliest phase, the Lower Palaeolithic (roughly 2 1/2 million to 150,000 years ago), stone tools were manufactured in the simplest way: direct blows from another stone struck off flakes; the simple shapes that resulted are the characteristic products of early hominids, including *Homo habilis* and *Homo erectus*. The discovery of Lower Palaeolithic tools in lands outside Africa is the most important evidence that we have of early hominid migrations.

During the second major phase, the Middle Palaeolithic (150,000 to 30,000 years ago), stone tools were produced from simple flakes by early members of our own species, including *Homo neanderthalensis* (the Neanderthals) and *Homo sapiens fossilis*, an early form of anatomically modern human.

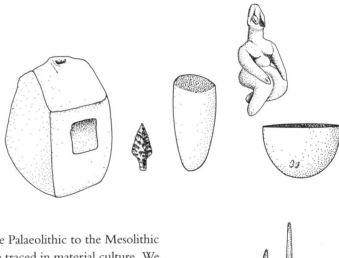

2.2   The transition from the Palaeolithic to the Mesolithic and Neolithic periods can be traced in material culture. We have uncovered more artifacts from the later periods both because older things are less likely to be preserved and because of the underlying economic reality: the Neolithic culture was based on agriculture and settled village life, so its people built more substantial structures and had a greater variety of tools and equipment than the Palaeolithic and Mesolithic peoples, who were foragers and traveled lightly. *From the bottom up*: a Palaeolithic chopper (stone tool); Mesolithic microlith and bone fish hooks; and Neolithic house, arrowhead, axe, figurine, and pot.

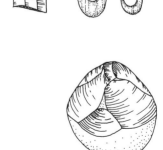

The third phase, the Upper Palaeolithic (30,000 to 13,000 years ago), is dominated by finely worked stone tools made on long thin flakes known as blades. Upper Palaeolithic stone-tool complexes, or industries, are usually associated with anatomically modern humans of our own species. All three phases of the Palaeolithic are represented in finds from Greece, although never in any great abundance, and everywhere with gaps in our knowledge or interruptions in the record of evidence.

The first certain evidence for the presence of hominids in Greece was discovered in a cave called Petralona on the Chalkidike peninsula near the northern city of Thessaloniki. The discovery was made in 1959 by local villagers looking for water; they found instead a fossilized cranium (a skull without the lower jaw) cemented in a stalagmite deep in a large cavern (see Figure 2.3). The heavily fossilized cranium appears to have belonged to a very unlucky individual. Ever since scientists described and published a picture of the skull in 1960, it has raised more questions than it has answered. How old is it? What species is it? And how did it get into the cavern where it was found?

The cranium is a lonely, isolated find. Although the cavern deposits have been explored by amateur paleontologists, there are few published facts to go by. The cavern is too dark and wet for habitation, and the numerous fossilized animal bones in the deposits are dominated by species such as the extinct cave hyena and cave bear, animals unlikely to have been congenial roommates for these hominids.

Two major theories account for the cranium's presence in the cavern. The theory with the most credibility is that it was brought into the cavern with the rest of the body by hyenas, which have a habit

2.3 The fossilized cranium from Petralona is an early form of human, perhaps *Homo heidelbergensis*, or perhaps an archaic form of *Homo sapiens*, who lived between 200,000 and 400,000 years ago.

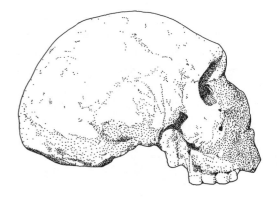

of dragging carcasses into their cave dens for leisurely eating. The smaller bones of the skeleton would have been broken up by the powerful jaws of the hyenas for their marrow, leaving only splinters, which have not survived. The more solid bones of the cranium may be the reason for its survival, abandoned on the floor of the den with the other debris of hyena meals.

The second hypothesis is more speculative. Other isolated finds of fossil hominid crania are known from caves in many other European countries (especially Spain, France, and Italy), and these crania may have been deliberately deposited by hominids in some kind of burial or other ceremonial practice. The problem with this hypothesis is that it is difficult to test. The evidence for hyena activity at Petralona is supported by the numerous remains of extinct Pleistocene hyenas and the animal bones they brought into the cavern. Since their habit of eating the long bones and leaving skulls can be reconstructed from the habits of living hyenas, we favor the first hypothesis.

The questions of age and species are even more difficult to answer. The stalagmite crust on the Petralona cranium was dated to 160,000 to 240,000 years ago with a geologic technique that uses radioactive isotopes of uranium and thorium, which occur naturally in the limestone cavern. The dripping water that formed the stalagmite crust on the cranium could only begin to accumulate after the skull was deposited on the cavern floor, so we can conclude that the fossil must be somewhat older than its stalagmitic covering. But how much older? The consensus of the expert paleontologists who have examined the fossil is that it probably dates to between 300,000 and 400,000 years ago. Until other specimens are found, or other techniques of dating fossils are developed, we must accept this guess.

Speculations about the species of the Petralona cranium are on the thinnest ice. It appears to be a member of a group sometimes called simply "archaic *Homo sapiens*" and sometimes "*Homo heidelbergensis*" because of its affinities with an isolated fossil human jaw discovered in Germany in the nineteenth century. Whatever name we use, its position in the history of human evolution is thought to be somewhere between *Homo erectus*, the first hominid to migrate out of Africa, and *Homo neanderthalensis*, the early human that dominated Europe and the Near East before the advent of our own species. The uncertainty is justified because the Petralona cranium has characteristics of both species. Its archaic characteristics are the projecting face, the heavy ridge of bone over the eye sockets, and the receding forehead, like the earlier *Homo erectus*; its more "modern" characteristics, which resemble those of the later *Homo sapiens*, include the large braincase, which is higher and rounder than that of the more primitive hominids. We prefer the appellation *Homo heidelbergensis*, although it has not yet been universally accepted, because it places the lonely Petralona cranium in its own class and recognizes its distinctive features.

Fortunately, this one fossil is not the only evidence available for tracing the migration of early hominids in Greece. At "open-air" sites, stone tools have been found directly on the present-day surface of the earth or only slightly beneath it. These were prehistoric campsites or perhaps tool-making sites, where the chief finds are shaped, or knapped, flint tools. After a campsite was abandoned in the distant past, the stone tools resisted the corrosion and decay that reduced other artifacts to dust and were in their turn buried by erosional sediments from higher ground, gradually encased in thickening layers of soil as the result of weathering and chemical action, or sometimes buried and reexposed repeatedly in the geologically active environment of Greece. Stone-tool sites are found chiefly in the northern and western districts (such as Thessaly and Epirus), although other parts of Greece undoubtedly have sites awaiting discovery.

Open-air sites are difficult to detect because they are often made up of no more than 30–40 stone artifacts scattered on the surface of an area as small as 20–30 meters on a side. This is the norm. A few very large and rich sites have produced thousands of lithic (stone) artifacts, but most sites are small, and the lithic artifacts are often difficult to distinguish from ordinary rocks (see Figure 2.4). Fewer than a hundred such sites are known at present.

Although everything from satellite imagery and aerial photography to hand-operated augers has been used to find them, the most successful technique is still the simplest. The search for early sites first requires the careful analysis of the geology of the region to identify sediments and soils that are of sufficient age to contain Palaeolithic sites (recent river alluvium, for instance, is not productive); then the researcher walks every ravine, roadcut, and river terrace in the right areas looking for places where erosion or recent digging has brought stone tools to the surface.

Only about a dozen Lower Palaeolithic sites have been identified by finds of stone tools. In 1987 and 1991 in Thessaly near the city of Larisa, we turned up half a dozen sites along the Peneios River and

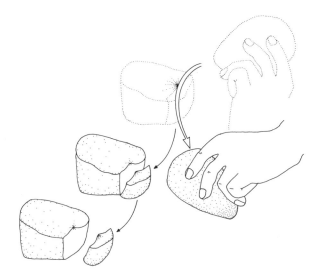

2.4   Prehistoric stone tools were manufactured by flintknapping. Brittle rocks such as flint, jasper, and obsidian were flaked by striking the edges with a stone or antler hammer. The core, or the block being flaked, can itself become a tool such as a hand-axe or chopper. The sharp flakes that are knocked off could be shaped into a variety of tools by flaking the edges, a process called "retouching."

in the hills to the south. These findspots, as we termed them, are all open-air sites marked by abundant artifacts manufactured from a lustrous white form of massive quartz. Most of the forms are simple flakes fashioned by chipping into scraping and cutting tools and some heavier pounding or chopping tools. One of the oldest known archaeological sites is at Rodia, on the Peneios River in Thessaly (see Figure 2.5).

Because few bones or other organic materials are present in the acid-rich deposits that contain the artifacts, we are uncertain how these sites were used or what we can learn from them. Just dating them is difficult. The fossils they contain, a few fossil animal bones in related deposits, and the general geological contexts of the sites suggest they were in use 300,000 to 400,000 years ago. They probably represent, therefore, the type of campsite left by highly mobile foragers, namely *Homo heidelbergensis*, who shifted their camps frequently in response to the seasonal availability of plants and animals. There were very few humans, after all, in a large landscape, and they had no need to stay put and intensively exploit a small portion of it, but were able to range widely in search of their favorite foods. At the very least, they offer tangible evidence of the presence of hominids, like the one at Petralona, in Greece at a very early date.

We found similar sites in the western province of Epirus in the early 1990s, one of which produced a typical pointed hand-axe that links the Greek sites to similar ones in the Near East and Europe (see

2.5   Rodia, in Thessaly. The layers of this site on the Peneios River are
gravel beds laid down by the river more than 300,000 years ago. Stone tools
are found at the level indicated by the hammer. The site was probably a
seasonal hunting camp on the banks of the river, which has since cut down
its bed by more than fifteen meters and left this terrace high and dry.

2.6   We discovered this large hand-axe at the site of Kokkinopilos in
Epirus in 1991. It dates to approximately 250,000 B.P. and is similar to
pointed hand-axes found at other European sites. This artifact is evidence
that Greece at this time was part of a large geographic region inhabited
by mobile foragers, probably an archaic form of *Homo sapiens* such as the
Neanderthals, *Homo heidelbergensis*, or *Homo erectus*.

Figure 2.6). Recently we identified Palaeolithic sites in Greek Macedonia while working with a Thessaloniki University team just north
of the Petralona cavern.

Scientists are somewhat surprised by the relatively late dates for the
Lower Palaeolithic sites in Greece, given the early date at which tool-
using hominids appeared in Africa and the early sites in adjacent re-

gions such as Spain (800,000 years ago) and the Near East (more than
1 million years ago). Although the more southern reaches of Europe
and the Near East that were adjacent to Africa were probably colonized by African hominids at very early dates, the fluctuating and
highly seasonal climate of continental and Mediterranean Europe in
the Ice Age may have deterred would-be colonists. How would hominid foragers, who were adapted to the relatively seasonless conditions
of plant growth and the limited migrations of animals in the equator-
ial latitudes, have coped with a good stiff European winter during a
period of glacial advance?

That hominids had migrated to Greece 400,000 years ago or later
is either the result of changing technology or cognitive abilities of
the hominids (remember the larger, rounder Petralona cranium), or
the result of hominids taking advantage of a relatively long period of
temperate conditions during or between periods of major glaciation.
The only thing we can say with certainty is that Greece was first inhabited, and then only minimally, at the tail end of the period of great
human migration that brought hominids from Africa to the Eurasian
continent.

The Middle Palaeolithic Period

Many more sites reveal a later phase of the Palaeolithic, when new
tool types succeeded the older, more primitive forms and presumably
a new type of human was on the scene. We know of only one fossilized skull from this period (found in a weathered sea cave on the
Mani peninsula of southern Greece and hence without a useful context). It may represent the Neanderthals (*Homo neanderthalensis*), who
were otherwise widespread after about 250,000 years ago in Europe,
parts of Russia, the Caucasus, the Near East, and North Africa west to
Morocco. We can only assume that the Neanderthals are responsible
for the many Middle Palaeolithic sites in almost every district of Greece
for which we have reliable information.

More than a hundred open-air sites have been detected from Thrace
and Macedonia in the extreme north to the southern reaches of the
Peloponnese. Middle Palaeolithic artifacts have also been discovered
on the lower levels of at least five excavated caves and rock shelters.
These finds are sufficient to show that the Middle Palaeolithic and
presumably the Neanderthals were widespread and very successful.
They were long-lasting too, from before about 150,000 B.P. (before

present) or even earlier in Epirus to as recently as 30,000 B.P. at sites near Larisa, Thessaly.

Middle Palaeolithic sites, both open-air and caves, are more systematically distributed than those of the Lower Palaeolithic. They appear to be closely tied to perennial sources of water from the seaside to the mountain valleys of the interior, suggesting that the Stone Age people studied the landscape and took a careful, logical approach to exploiting its resources. The stone tools are distinctive also. The Middle Palaeolithic industry is usually called Mousterian (after the site of Le Moustier in France, where they were first identified) and consists of small thin flakes of flint that have been carefully chipped ("retouched" in archaeological jargon). The variety of tool types is more numerous and the tools more consistent than in any earlier industry. The new tool types include cutting and scraping tools, along with gravers, borers, and spear points that bear the marks of hafting and the damaged tips characteristic of use (see Figure 2.9). They are typical for

2.7 Palaeolithic foragers were particularly attracted to places with water. In the Pleistocene epoch Greece was as dry as it is today, perhaps even drier. Permanent water sources such as the Peneios River in Thessaly and Lake Kopais in Boeotia were natural magnets for plants, birds, animals, and the early foragers who preyed on them. In Epirus, natural basins in the limestone, eroded out by thousands of years of rain, filled with clay that drifted in and eventually became shallow, seasonal lakes that provided important foraging opportunities, particularly during a long, dry, glacial summer.

the foragers of the Middle Palaeolithic, who appear to have specialized in hunting big game such as bison and aurochs (wild oxen) and, to judge by bones from some sites in Greece, rhinoceros and even elephant. We must assume that they also used the other resources of this landscape, collecting plant foods such as nuts, fruit, and mushrooms. When other game was scarce they could collect fish, frogs, and waterfowl in abundance at the water sources where they made their camps (see Figure 2.7).

Some readers may think of prehistory as a period during which human mental and technological progress evolved continuously and therefore expect to read about more or less constant change in the archaeological record. But we take a view more in line with the historian Thucydides, who expected human nature at some level to persist through the ages, at least after the emergence of the distinctively modern form of human consciousness, whenever and wherever that may have happened. In our opinion, the Neanderthals of Greece exhibit a fully modern mentality, using the land much as foragers in later ages would do, suggesting no great difference in their cognitive abilities or limitations in their technology or environmental adaptation. An argument could be made that the Neanderthals might have persisted indefinitely if the environmental conditions they were familiar with had continued as well. Their disappearance and the transition from the Middle Palaeolithic to the last phase of the Old Stone Age must be explained by circumstances that forced the change rather than some inexorable dynamic of change (see Figure 2.8).

There is no question, however, that the Neanderthals disappeared. The distinctive Mousterian stone tools and the many sites where they were found appear to have lingered on in Greece until quite late, about 30,000 B.P., but then they vanish, abruptly, completely, and permanently. From the very moment of the discovery of the first Neanderthal fossil in Germany over 140 years ago, scientists have questioned the relationship of the Neanderthals to modern humans. At first they were thought to be too primitive to be a direct ancestor, particularly because of their large faces, heavy brow ridges, and receding foreheads. But by the beginning of the twentieth century they were becoming accepted as our ancestors on the basis of the growing body of evidence from European sites that they buried their dead, successfully adapted to the glacial conditions of the late Pleistocene, and used sophisticated tools. The new tool types include cutting and scraping tools, along with gravers, borers, and spear points that bear the marks of hafting and the damaged tips characteristic of use (see Figure 2.9).

This view was dealt a blow by the research of the anatomist Marcellin Boule in the early twentieth century, who argued that the skeletal structure and primitive skull of the Neanderthal were too unlike modern humans for there to be any direct connections. This seemingly definitive conclusion persisted for half a century and is incidentally responsible for fostering the hard-to-root-out view of Neanderthals in cartoons and jocular speech as burly, barbarous buffoons.

Much more archaeological evidence continued to accumulate, however, all of it pointing to the sophisticated and complex behavior of the Neanderthals. Flowers were buried with a corpse in the Shanidar Cave of Iraq; cave bear bones were ceremonially arranged in piles or in buried caches in European caves; and there was mounting evidence that Neanderthals cared for the sick and aged members of their bands, all evidence of distinctly human behavior. By the time of the centennial in 1959 of the publication of Darwin's *On the Origin of*

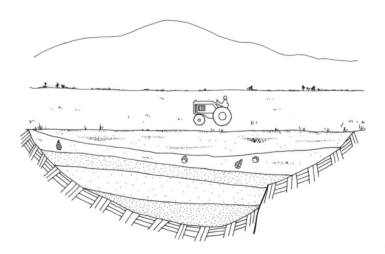

2.8   The lakes vanished when the limestone basins of Epirus (technically known as karst features) were completely filled with sediments. Today, ancient lakes are visible only as darker layers in eroded sections through the old karst features far below the modern surface of the land. Because many early sites in Greece are deeply buried by later sediments or are associated with the fossil terrace systems of ancient rivers, they are hard to locate and identify, and even more difficult to investigate scientifically. This is one reason the earlier Stone Age period is not well known in Greece.

Species, the archaeological evidence was combined with the anatomical investigation of newly discovered Neanderthal skeletons to once again proclaim the Neanderthals direct ancestors and even to reclassify them as *Homo sapiens neanderthalensis*. They were kissing cousins, so to speak. It may not surprise the reader to learn that this orthodoxy has again been questioned, and since 1987 there has been a growing movement among scientists to once more remove the Neanderthals from our own lineage.

The movement began with the application of a new technique called thermoluminescence, which can be used to date burned flints. The dates revealed two surprising things. The first was that anatomically modern fossil human remains from the Qafzeh Cave in Israel were up to 100,000 years old. The second was that classic Neanderthals at the nearby Kebara Cave were only 60,000 years old or less. The inescapable conclusion is that these obvious representatives of our

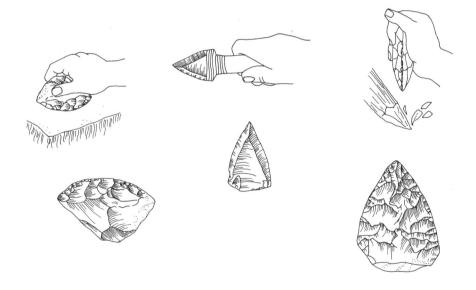

2.9   Sites of the Middle Palaeolithic period in Greece are marked, as elsewhere in Europe and the Near East, by abundant stone tools belonging to the industry traditionally known as Mousterian (named after the site of Le Moustier in France). Mousterian tools were probably made by archaic forms of early humans such as Neanderthals and include scrapers for working hides, heavy-duty cutting tools such as small hand-axes and choppers for cutting wood and bone, and numerous pointed forms that were hafted onto short thrusting spears for hunting.

own species overlapped with classic Neanderthalers both chronologically and geographically for more than 40,000 years. The *simultaneous* existence of these two different hominid stocks must mean that they belong to two distinct species, and hence Neanderthals must again be relegated to the status of dead-end losers. This conclusion has been reinforced by tests of the surviving DNA from the original Neanderthal specimen found in Germany in 1856. It had been shellacked, and the sealed fossils still preserved some DNA material, which, when studied, was found to be sufficiently different from the DNA of living humans to place the Neanderthals in an entirely separate group.

And what does this mean about the disappearance of the Neanderthals in Greece? Our evidence fits well with the new model of separate species. Current thinking has modern forms of *Homo sapiens* making their appearance first in Africa (where else?) more than 200,000 years ago, and then migrating to the Near East where they first came into contact with their archaic cousins, the Neanderthals. For thousands of years the two groups appear to have occupied more or less the same ground, until about 50,000 years ago when *Homo sapiens* began once more to move.

A clear pattern of extensive migrations on a continental scale brought our direct ancestors to Asia, Australia, Japan, and ultimately the New World itself. Closer to Greece, the movement of the modern humans can be followed across Asia Minor to the Balkans and into Europe. The line of march is littered with the stone tools, bone spear points, and other artifacts that we call "Aurignacian" (after yet another site in France) and that belong properly to the Upper Palaeolithic (see Figure 2.10). The Aurignacian artifacts are distinctly different from the Mousterian, and what is more, Aurignacian sites are progressively younger the farther west they are: 50,000 B.P. in the Near East, 45,000 B.P. in the Balkans, and 35,000 B.P. in western Europe. This chronological pattern is strong evidence of the migration, or as archaeologists prefer to call it, the demic diffusion, of a new people, *Homo sapiens,* that displaced and ultimately replaced the Neanderthalers throughout their geographic range.

Unknown are the forces that set our ancestors in motion after many thousands of years of status quo, driving them to wander the land and waterways of the world, to brave the rigors of the Arctic in crossing to the New World, to replace the archaic humans in their path. That circumstance, namely a largely uninhabited earth with two or more different species of humans coexisting in a small part of it, had no precedent and will never occur again. In local terms, however, the late survival of Neanderthals in Spain, Italy, and as we have argued, Greece, until about 30,000 years ago suggests that the Neanderthals were pushed or retreated into the remote southern peninsulas of Europe, cut off from the main continent and from each other by the spreading populations of modern *Homo sapiens*. The disappearance of the Mousterian and Neanderthal fossils from the archaeological record after this time speaks for itself: the race was won by modern humans, and the Neanderthals became extinct. We may never know whether the Neanderthals' disappearance was due to direct conflict with the new species, the collapse of viable breeding populations, or some other factor such as disease. Whatever theory we prefer or pursue, the outcome was the same for the unfortunate Neanderthals who met their fate on the banks of the Peneios River in Thessaly.

The Upper Palaeolithic

We know for certain that modern humans were in possession of Greece by 30,000 years ago. The details of the transition from the Middle to the Upper Palaeolithic, from Neanderthals to modern humans, remain to be worked out. Our own research from the banks of the Bosphorus Strait in northwestern Turkey to the shore of the Ionian Sea in western Greece has turned up evidence of Aurignacian sites typical of those known in the Near East and the Balkans. Within

2.10   The arrival of anatomically modern *Homo sapiens* in the Balkans is signaled by the appearance of a distinctly different stone tool industry called Aurignacian. Tools were retouched from slender blades, like the one in the hand, or on the ends of long flakes, as seen on the right. Typical forms include the knifelike blade, rounded scrapers for hide-working on the ends of the flakes, and a chisel-ended graving tool (burin) marked with a small arrow. Burins were used to work antler, bone, and wood to fashion tools and weapons with slots that could be set with sharp flints to form knives and spears.

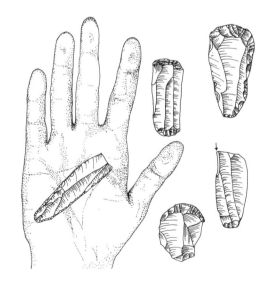

Greece proper, 150,000 stone tools have been found at the large Aurignacian surface site of Spilaion at the mouth of the Acheron River in Epirus. Smaller sites have been found in the northern Peloponnese in Achaia and in caves in the Argolid. Although the sites are very few in number, their locations appear to have no connection with the land-use strategies of the Neanderthals.

The earliest Aurignacian settlers were indeed few and far between, and apart from the probable long-term base camps at sites such as Spilaion (and perhaps Franchthi Cave in the Argolid), they left no network of sites that marked the strategic use of widespread resources in the Middle Palaeolithic. They appear instead to have concentrated on a few choice areas, leaving other parts of the landscape entirely empty.

This peculiar pattern of discontinuous settlement, which is widely recognized in the Balkans as a "patchiness" in the archaeological record, is difficult to understand. There are very few documented Upper Palaeolithic sites of the Aurignacian or later phases dated before 26,000 B.P., and even after this date, when we otherwise have a number of well-documented sites, some regions continued to be ignored. Our own surveys in Thessaly and Macedonia have turned up no Upper Palaeolithic activity after this date, in sharp contrast with the Argolid and Epirus, where sites are relatively numerous. Perhaps we should blame the deteriorating glacial climate, which led to a sharply colder and drier climate peaking about 20,000 B.P. Pollen cores from lakes and marshes in Greece have shown that the landscape became progressively treeless, eventually to be dominated by steppe vegetation such as artemesia (a kind of sagebrush) and grasses. The vegetation would have supported large herds of wild animals, particularly bison, aurochs, and horses, all prey animals for Upper Palaeolithic hunters.

So why is there no evidence that these hunters expanded their activities inland? The most likely explanation is that the hunters and foragers preferred the coastal plains, which were exposed when sea levels dropped by as much as 150 meters as sea water was taken up in large glacial polar icecaps. These coastal shelves became plains that provided a sheltered, warmer, and perhaps preferable habitat for humans and animals alike. In contrast, the interior of the Greek peninsula, today the only remaining dry land, would then have been a dry and cold place in the glacial winter, useful only in the short summer season for specialized hunting and plant-collecting forays.

There is some support for this hypothesis in the distribution and character of the known Upper Palaeolithic sites. The Upper Palaeolithic after 26,000 B.P. has been investigated by excavations at a number of sites, the best known ones being in Epirus (Asprochaliko Cave, Kastritsa Cave, Klithi Cave), Corfu (Grava Cave), the Argolid (Kephalari Cave, Klisoura Cave, Franchthi Cave), Boeotia (Seidi Cave), and Thessaly (Theopetra Cave). None of these caves—actually shallow rock shelters—are of any great depth, except Franchthi and Kephalari, which are true caverns (see Figure 2.11). In other words they are very small sites. The artifacts found in them are evidence of the highly specialized activities that took place there. Most were well away from the sea in the interior (again, Kephalari and Franchthi are the exceptions since they were within ten kilometers of the coast), situated in such a way as to suggest that they were special-purpose camps located in good hunting grounds.

Asprochaliko and Kastritsa Caves are typical Upper Palaeolithic sites. Both were discovered and excavated in the 1960s by Eric Higgs of the University of Cambridge and have been studied more recently by a team directed by G. N. Bailey of the University of Newcastle-

2.11 Many of the sites occupied by Palaeolithic foragers are nothing more than small rock shelters, hollowed out by rainwater running over the soft limestone bedrock. These simple overhangs provided valuable shelter from winter rain and summer sun. The present-day floors, often covered with droppings from sheep and goats that take shelter in such places, conceal the many layers that testify to long periods of use.

upon-Tyne. Asprochaliko has two main periods. The Middle Palaeolithic is at the base of the deposits and is characterized by tools made on large flakes of flint. The upper levels are separated from the underlying Middle Palaeolithic layers by a hiatus in the deposits of unknown length; they contain evidence of a stone-tool industry dominated by small "backed" blades (blades on which one edge is blunted by retouching) used as projectile points. The abundant animal bones in the site include such large herbivores as bison and aurochs, and even traces of exotic animals such as rhinoceros. Located on the side of a narrow ravine carved out by the Louros River, the cave has long been viewed as a useful campsite for hunters who followed the herds on their annual migrations. G. N. Bailey suggests that a favorite tactic was to ambush the game on the plateau above the cave and in the valleys parallel to the river.

Kastritsa Cave is located south of the city of Ioannina overlooking Lake Pamvotis, which was much larger in the Pleistocene when the cave was inhabited. A deposit of sand in the excavations records the high-water mark. Higgs found that this very small shelter had Upper Palaeolithic deposits spanning the period from 26,000 to 13,000 years ago. At a much higher elevation than Asprochaliko, Kastritsa appears to have been a summer campsite for foragers in transit from the coastal plains to the highlands. The fauna hunted there were different from those at Asprochaliko farther to the south, as are the stone tools found there (a large number of distinctive shouldered arrowheads and spearpoints). These differences are explained by the difference in seasonal hunting practices at the two caves.

Klithi is perhaps the best example of a very specialized site. The cave is located in a high mountain gorge of the Voidomatis River north of Ioannina, near enough to the ancient line of Pleistocene glaciers to have been uninhabitable except in relatively mild periods of climate, and then only in the summer months after the snowpack had melted. Klithi was excavated in the 1980s by G. N. Bailey, who found a specialized assemblage of backed blades and highly fragmentary bones and horns; these were likely left by small seasonal work parties who harvested mountain ibex, a species of wild mountain goat.

Other caves, such as Theopetra (in Thessaly) and Seidi (in Boeotia), are located deep in the interior on the margins of rivers and lakes. The Klisoura sites in the Argolid were close to the now-vanished Lake Lerna, and Grava Cave (on Corfu) may have overlooked a large area of streams and estuaries on the western coast of the island. All of these

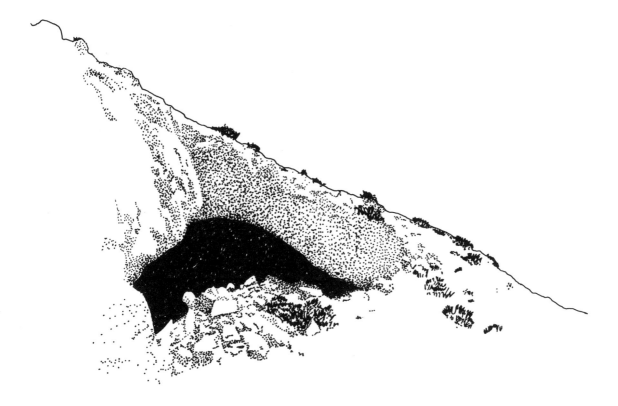

2.12   Franchthi Cave in the southern Argolid is one of the few proper caves to be inhabited in Greece. The site was excavated by an Indiana University team directed by Thomas W. Jacobsen from 1967 to 1979. It contains evidence of intermittent occupation from the Middle Palaeolithic through the end of the Neolithic period, or roughly from 35,000 to 5000 B.P., making it a valuable source of information for the entire Stone Age.

caves may have been way stations between the mountains and the coastal plains. Only Kephalari and Franchthi are extensive caverns capable of holding large numbers of people. Their proximity to the sea today suggests that they could have been base camps. But appearances can be deceiving.

If the sea were lowered to its level during the last glacial period, the Argolic Gulf would be empty, leaving Franchthi and Kephalari high and dry. Although the findings from Kephalari have not been published in detail, the Franchthi Cave excavations have shown that the Upper Palaeolithic occupation was small and periodic (see Figure 2.12). The chief finds are small backed blades of flint used to tip spears, darts, and arrows. These weapons were associated with fireplaces and the bones of large animals such as wild ass, bison, aurochs, and elk. Little evidence has been found that the people used plants for food, and there are no graves, no artworks, and no permanent constructions such as hearths or walls.

The phases of occupation appear to have been short and often interrupted; the whole picture is similar to that seen at the smaller rock shelters. The known caves and shelters were likely short-term camps used by small groups of foragers—we think typically no more than a dozen—as hunting stations on their seasonal treks from the coastal base camps to the cool, lush grasses of the mountain meadows of the interior.

The end of the Upper Palaeolithic phase marks the end of the Old Stone Age proper. Many proponents of evolutionary change assume that the transition from the Upper Palaeolithic to the following Mesolithic and Neolithic periods was one of uninterrupted cultural evolution and technological progress. But again the picture is clouded with uncertainty. Discontinuous sequences, and sometimes a technological reversal, with a return to more primitive stone tools and an impoverished material culture, dominate the record. If one embraces, as we do, a view of human history as one of nonprogressive change within a field of relatively stable physical and mental characteristics, this picture is perhaps not surprising.

The facts are these: with only one significant exception, namely Franchthi Cave, all of the known caves inhabited in the Upper Palaeolithic were abandoned at the end of the Pleistocene era around 13,000–14,000 B.P. Most were never used again, or they were used only much later, after the Stone Age was over, by shepherds and Byzantine hermits.

An eerie silence falls over the archaeological record at the time when the last Ice Age gives way to the modern climatic conditions of the Holocene epoch. A traveler sailing along the Greek coastline after the ice caps melted and the sea had risen to its present-day height would have seen wooded slopes and plains devoid of people, inhabited only by wild boar and deer, with sea birds, seals, and turtles massed on the shore. As dusk fell, all would be dark in the mountain valleys, where for so many thousands of years the flicker of firelight had lighted the shelters in the rock with a soft orange glow. Only a few shiny flints and rapidly moldering slivers of bone remained to mark the homes of generations of souls.

An explanation for this reversal of fortune is difficult to find. Although the base camps on the coastal plains were submerged by the rising sea as the glaciers melted, and the inland valleys and hills were quickly covered by an expanding forest of deciduous oak and pine, these changes should have presented no difficulty for a resourceful people. In the northern and western parts of Atlantic Europe foragers quickly adjusted to the new climatic conditions and lived there for thousands of years into the Holocene era. Perhaps in Greece the population was simply too small to pursue the old ways of life. Some groups followed the herds of bison and aurochs that migrated north to the open plains of southeastern Europe and the steppes of Russia. The population grew ever smaller, and eventually people were so few and far between that their presence is virtually undetectable by the archaeological techniques that we have at our disposal.

THE MESOLITHIC PERIOD

Beginning about 16,000 B.P., as the climate rapidly turned warmer and wetter, the last Ice Age broke up. The great glaciers retreated, and the level of the oceans around the world rose dramatically in response to the vast quantities of meltwater. By 10,000 B.P. the world had once again entered a warm interglacial era: the current climatic regime, the Holocene. After 30,000 years of great cold and very dry conditions, the return to a warmer and wetter climate brought about major shifts in the very shape of the land and had profound effects on populations of animals and plants. Greece was molded by the new climate conditions.

Once again the westerlies from the Atlantic brought winter rains, and forests of deciduous oak and pine moved out of sheltered river valleys to colonize the stable Pleistocene soils that cloaked the land. Most of the big Pleistocene animals such as elephants, bison, aurochs, wild ass, ibex, and antelope either migrated north to the southern Russian plain following the retreat of the steppes or became extinct. Species adapted to forested environments thrived. The Mesolithic faunal remains found in the Franchthi Cave are dominated by elk, deer, and pigs, all typical forest species.

The most dramatic change was the alteration in the shoreline brought about by the rise of sea level on the coastal plains. The rise was rapid. From a low level of over 100 meters at the end of the

Pleistocene, it rose to 50 meters about 11,000 B.P. and to 20 meters at 8000 B.P. Some low plains were drowned as the seas rose; shallow places lost many kilometers of coastal plain. The change would have been fast enough for contemporary humans to see their traditional hunting grounds disappearing.

The loss of coastal plain brought the sea to the mouth of the Franchthi Cave in three or four thousand years; its distance from the coast was reduced from five to seven kilometers to one. The cave lost its best territory in the twinkling of an eye in geologic terms (see Figure 2.13).

In other regions the changes were just as marked: Early in the Holocene, Corfu was cut off from the mainland, and the Cycladic landmass in the Aegean broke up into islands, establishing the approximate present coastal configuration. Although sea level has continued to rise to the present day, changes in the shape of the land have been

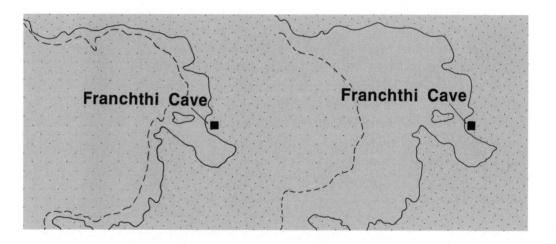

2.13 The coastline near Franchthi Cave has changed position considerably in the past 14,000 years. During the glacial maximum (ca. 20,000 B.P.), when the sea level was considerably lower because so much water was frozen in the polar ice caps, the coastline was several kilometers west of the cave. A large coastal plain crossed by rivers existed at this time (*right*). Since the end of the Ice Age, approximately 14,000 years ago, the ice caps have melted, sea level has risen, and the coastline moved eastward until it reached its present position just below the mouth of the cave after Roman times (*left*). The loss of the fertile coastal plain during this period seriously compromised the value of the cave for its human inhabitants.

relatively minor in the past five to six thousand years. The damage was done early. The coastal plains lost to the sea were the best and most productive habitats: relatively low-lying and sheltered in the Pleistocene, with abundant water, wooded streams and rivers, and good grazing for animals. The loss of this habitat pushed humans back onto the more rugged and rocky higher elevations of the interior, where water was scarce in the Mediterranean dry season, the new forests made movement difficult, and hunting was a less reliable source of food. There were some compensations, of course; the rapid rise in sea level created swamps, coastal lagoons, and estuaries that teemed with wildlife. There was plenty of food, but of an entirely different kind.

As we have already noted, during the hiatus in the occupation of prehistoric Greece, the country was abandoned, or at least the Palaeolithc foragers retreated to refuges where we have not been able to detect them. Perhaps we should have expected this change. As our own surveys have shown, the Palaeolithic hunters operated in only a few regions of the country, and excavations have revealed numerous large and small interruptions or hiatuses in the occupation of even the largest sites (such as Franchthi Cave) in the period between 30,000 and 13,000 B.P.

Of the many possible hypotheses that could account for this phenomenon, we believe it was likely the loss of habitat. Foragers in the Old Stone Age needed immense tracts of territory to support an economy based on wild plants and animals, something on the order of about 600 square kilometers for the average band of 50 to 75 people. In the late Pleistocene humans probably concentrated on the best and most productive portions of the landscape whenever they could. And there were never very many of them to begin with. Population levels are hard to estimate, and the uncertainties in the calculations are great, but if we consider the size of the territory available—subtracting the higher mountainous lands and areas known to be uninhabited, adding the coastal plains, and allowing at least 600 square kilometers for each band—the total number of humans in Greece was on the order of 4,000 to 7,000 individuals. The loss of large parts of the best territory to forest and the incursion of the sea would also have reduced the number of traditional Palaeolithic foragers. The population could quickly have reached an unsustainably low level.

If prehistoric archaeology teaches us anything, it is that human beings are both curious and persistent. Greece may have reverted for centuries or even a couple of millennia to its natural state before the first appearance of humans, but it was not to last. Early in the Holocene, approximately 12,000 years ago or a millennium after the Palaeolithic, a new people in some ways very different from their predecessors made their debut. Unlike earlier migrants who came by land, they came from across the sea.

Our best evidence for reconstructing life in the Mesolithic, as this new period is called, comes from Franchthi Cave, which was excavated between 1967 and 1979 by Thomas W. Jacobsen of Indiana University. The Mesolithic there begins abruptly after a hiatus thought to have lasted about 900 years. The new habitation layers contain stone tools that are completely different from those of the Palaeolithic (see Figure 2.14).

The earliest Mesolithic stone tools at Franchthi are small flakes, often about the size of a fingernail, which were chipped into simple scraping tools with crude notches or "teeth" for rough woodworking tasks. In the centuries that followed, the most notable development was the reappearance of geometric microliths (similar tools were made by a different technique in the Palaeolithic) made by a complex technique of flaking small pieces of flint into geometric shapes such as

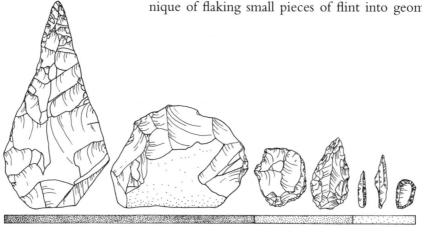

2.14   The succession of Palaeolithic stone tools is not progressive, but shows many large and small changes. The larger tools on the left are the typical core tools of the Lower Palaeolithic (Acheulean), the flake tools in the middle are Middle Palaeolithic (Mousterian), and the small pieces on the right belong to the Upper Palaeolithic of the Aurignacian and later. The shaded bars below them indicate the approximate, but proportional, length of the periods, with the Lower Palaeolithic lasting from 300,000 to 135,000 B.P., the Middle Palaeolithic from 135,000 to 30,000 B.P., and the Upper Palaeolithic from 30,000 to 13,000 B.P.

trapezoids and triangles. There is much archaeological and ethno-graphic evidence that these tiny tools were used as arrowheads (see Figure 2.15).

New forms of stone tools are not the only innovations seen in this period. For the first time anywhere in Greece, we have evidence that people buried their dead. In the mouth of the cave a number of graves

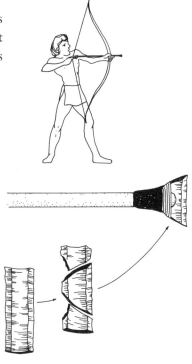

2.15   Mesolithic sites often produce small, geometrically shaped stone tools known as "microliths." In Greece microliths are typically trapezoidal in outline. They were retouched from small flakes or seg-ments of broken blades and mounted on the ends of reed arrowshafts. The broad cutting edge thus created was ideal for clipping the wings of waterfowl when fired into a flock of flying birds. Stone-tipped arrows of this type were so effective that Egyptian pharaohs continued to hunt with them thousands of years later.

2.16   The grave of this young male in his late twenties was found at Franchthi Cave. Dating to the Mesolithic period, it is the oldest deliberate burial site known in Greece. He was buried in a tightly flexed position in a shallow pit cut in the dark, ashy earth, rich in shell fragments, near the mouth of the cave, and then covered with a mound of small stones. Remains of other bodies, some belonging to women and very small children and infants, were found nearby and are evidence that this cave was permanently occupied at the time. Two of the bodies had been cremated. This is the first evidence of cremation in Greece.

were discovered, the most interesting of which was that of a young man about 29 years of age. He lay on his back with his legs folded up behind him and his hands over his chest. He was laid out on a bed of crushed shell and ash with a mound of stones heaped over his body. He died of a blow to the head, but the condition of his bones shows that he was suffering from anemia, perhaps the result of malaria, when he died, approximately 9,500 years ago (see Figure 2.16). The other graves, some of which are interments and others cremations, are of men, women, and children, evidence that whole families resided in the cave with enough permanence to protect their deceased relatives from scavengers and disturbance by natural agents.

These special features of the Franchthi Mesolithic community allow us to conclude that they were long-term occupants of the cave, and perhaps permanent residents. The carefully tended and protected graves, the provisioning of the site with imported grinding stones, and the presence of children all support this supposition. The first evidence of artistic expression is also found in this period. A few perforated pebbles decorated with enigmatic scratches, which were probably worn as pendants, were found at Franchthi. The Mesolithic period at Franchthi was very short—less than two millennia—yet the thick layers are rich with artifacts, and the evidence of social complexity is present from the very first phase of occupation.

Other significant changes are noticeable in the Mesolithic layers. Hunting was still important, with the main animals hunted being elk, deer, and wild boar, but for the first time we have solid evidence that the people also ate wild plants. Carbonized remains of wild barley, lentils, almonds, and pistachios are sufficiently numerous to show that plants were being brought into the cave, and the use of grains and seeds was great enough to require the importation of lava querns from the volcanic island of Aigina to crush them as part of food preparation.

Even more noteworthy was the addition of seafood to the diet, particularly when we consider how little fish and shellfish was eaten in the Palaeolithic. Cave deposits include shells and bones from pelagic (deep sea) species of fish such as tunny. The presence of large fish has been taken as evidence that the Franchthi people used boats, which have been tentatively identified as papyrus boats similar to the larger boats used on the Nile in the Bronze Age.

Decisive evidence of seafaring is provided by the obsidian tools that make up about 3 percent of the stone tools in the site. Obsidian is a volcanic glass found only on the Aegean islands, where volcanic eruptions created the right conditions (of magma chemistry and cooling) for its formation. Special physical and chemical tests of the Franchthi obsidian show that it originated on the Cycladic island of Melos, which was separated from Franchthi and the mainland of Greece by more than 100 kilometers of open sea. It could only be reached by boat. The seafaring Franchthi people probably collected the obsidian while they were on fishing expeditions, or possibly they received it in trade from other seafarers.

In an interesting experiment sponsored by the Museum of Nautical History in Piraeus, Greece, researchers constructed a papyrus boat based on the traditional design used by fisherman on the island of Corfu and in 1988 sailed it from Franchthi Cave to the obsidian source on Melos. At the very least they demonstrated that such a voyage was possible, and they also proved that the inhabitants of Franchthi could have utilized these simple materials to construct a seagoing vessel and could have successfully navigated the tricky seas among the Cyclades with such a craft (see Figure 2.17).

The Mesolithic people's interest in marine resources and use of boats is only one reason for assuming that they came from the sea. In

2.17   The obsidian found in the Mesolithic levels at Franchthi Cave came from the Cycladic island of Melos, more than a hundred kilometers away over open sea. Some kind of reed boat was probably used to cross the sea. This replica, constructed by a Corfiote boat maker using native papyrus, was sailed by members of a Greek marine historical society to Melos to prove that the ancient Mesolithic inhabitants of Greece were competent seafarers.

our view, there is a clear pattern of marine exploration and migration all across the Mediterranean in the early Holocene. Similarities in material culture (stone tools, burial practices) are rather general but suggest that the long coast stretching north from Palestine to southern Turkey was the point of departure for the mariners, a supposition supported by prevailing winds and currents and the timing of Mesolithic settlements (generally older in the eastern Mediterranean, less old in the Aegean, and even younger in western Greece).

The trip to Greece may have taken seafarers first to the big islands like Cyprus, where an early Holocene site has been found in association with many bones of the native pygmy hippopotami and mammoth. Likewise on Crete, the next likely landfall, hippos and elephants also perished in the early Holocene. The extinctions of these native Pleistocene fauna can be attributed to human predation and habitat destruction. The fauna had been isolated for hundreds of thousands of years, surviving on islands where there is no evidence of earlier Palaeolithic human habitation. Humans arrived in the Aegean islands only about 13,000 B.P. or slightly earlier, when Melian obsidian appeared at Palaeolithic Franchthi. As humans began sailing to the nearer islands, the native fauna of the bigger islands began to disappear. Their disappearance accelerated dramatically in the early Holocene.

In our model, the Mesolithic mariners represent a first wave of demic diffusion from the Near East to the southern margins of the European continent; this was followed by a larger wave of farmers in the next period. We cannot determine that the incentive for this seaborne migration was due to any problem in the homeland; more likely the mariners were drawn by the attractions of the Aegean islands and the Greek littoral. The barren, rocky, and waterless islands of the central Aegean today are largely devoid of plants and animals, but this was not always true.

In the early Holocene a wetter, warmer climate, as well as a lack of hunters and foragers, permitted these islands to teem with life. Safe from predators, large colonies of sea birds nested on the smaller islands, while turtles and seals hauled up on the beaches as they still do on one or two islands today. The rocks were encrusted with shellfish, and in deeper water dolphins, whales, and schools of immense deepwater fish thrived. The larger islands had indigenous fauna such as ibex, deer, and hares, as well as pygmy hippos and elephants. Like the dodo and carrier pigeon of recent memory, most of these animals have been cleared from their haunts by generations of hunters and fishers, a process that began in prehistory, accelerated after the advent of civilization, and has reached its evident conclusion in our own day. Animal populations that were not hunted or fished out were ultimately decimated by habitat loss from the Neolithic period on. Even more devastating, the destruction of indigenous plant species caused the collapse of the animal populations that depended on them for food.

All this lay in the future, however. In the early days of the Holocene the bounty of the islands and the Greek coast must have appeared boundless, and in the good sailing season we can envision small boats plying the waters of the eastern Mediterranean in search of new shores to exploit.

Franchthi Cave is one of the few Mesolithic sites in Greece, and the others are not as well known. Our own research has brought to light three Mesolithic sites in the Argolid and in 1993 another half-dozen on the western coast of Epirus. Most are located close to the coast. The only inland site is Theopetra in western Thessaly, discovered by our Greek colleagues, which has at least one human burial site like Franchthi's. The coastal sites are all small, consisting chiefly of flaked stone tools found on the surface. The newly discovered sites in Epirus are assumed to have been campsites in coastal sand dunes, and the presence of microlithic arrowheads suggests that they were seasonal hunting camps located at places where water was abundant. Mesolithic foragers likely sought out lagoons, tidal pools, and estuaries where wildfowl and aquatic animals were abundant.

Only one other Mesolithic site has been excavated. The site of Sidari on Corfu was excavated in the 1960s by Augustus Sordinas of the Ionian University of Corfu. Only the lowest layer of the site is Mesolithic; it dates to ca. 7700 – 8000 B.P. The site was an open-air settlement for foragers who concentrated on the shellfish and fish that abound in the cold waters there and in the straits between the island and the mainland. The deposits are made up of ash from campfires, and the midden of ash and other organic debris contains thousands of marine shells, as well as the bones of birds, small animals, and fish. The thousands of tools are microliths (small stone tools) with the trapezoidal arrowhead as one of the main elements. These simple tools were widely distributed around the Mediterranean and European shores and may have been diffused with the type of bow-and-arrow technology used by seafaring foragers. There are no burials at Sidari, and there is no evidence of permanent occupation, artwork, plant collecting, or any of the other features of complex life identified at Franchthi Cave. Here then is possibly a site typical of the average Mesolithic camp, representing the first beachhead established in northwestern Greece by the mariners of the Mediterranean.

These two excavated sites and the dozen sites known from surface survey are the only Mesolithic sites in Greece. Why is this so? Where are the others? The preference of these people for coastal sites may be part of the answer. Although the sea level rose only 20 to 40 meters during this period, it may have been enough to drown many sites on the coastal plain. Such small, ephemeral sites would be hard to locate for archaeologists, and difficult to excavate.

This first age of exploration and discovery in the Aegean was of vital importance because it prepared the way for the farmers who were to follow, bringing a radical new way of life that would shape the Greek countryside and economy into what we see today. About 9000 B.P. (as measured by radiocarbon assays of organic materials from sites such as Franchthi), new peoples made their appearance in eastern mainland Greece and the islands. These village-dwelling farmers, who grew wheat and barley and herded sheep and goats, abruptly replaced the foragers. The climate was essentially like today's, although perhaps warmer and wetter. Trees cloaked many hills, holding in place soils accumulated over tens of thousands of years. These forests were still rich in game, the lakes and rivers were full of wildfowl and fish, and the sea was rich in fish and other animals. Above all, the valleys and plains were covered with fertile, arable land that had never known the touch of the digging stick or the plow. But all that was soon to change.

CHAPTER THREE

THE NEW STONE AGE

The Earliest Greek Civilization

Sir John Lubbock coined the word "Neolithic" (New Stone Age) in 1865 in order to distinguish that archaeological period, in which polished stone axes and other stone tools that were ground into shape, from the Old Stone Age, in which flints were shaped by flaking. Lubbock's distinction was based solely on technological changes, but later prehistorians further differentiated the Old and New Stone Age by their economic practices as well. Today the Neolithic period properly understood is the age of the first village-dwelling farmers.

Farming is generally described as the production of food through the direct control of domesticated plants and animals. But this rather simple definition masks a complicated process that encompasses many activities and sometimes subtle relationships between humans and the plant and animal species they exploit. Experts today recognize that farming covers activities from the simple weeding and cultivating of wild plants and the selective culling of herds of wild animals to the full-scale genetic engineering of new species of plants and animals through selective breeding.

The earlier and simpler stages of cultivation are difficult to detect archaeologically, but the emergence of genetically transformed animal species is sometimes easily detected through the size and shape of animal bones, teeth, and horns, which often survive on archaeological sites. The genetic manipulation of food species, which is much in the public eye today, is nothing new under the sun. Selective breeding has

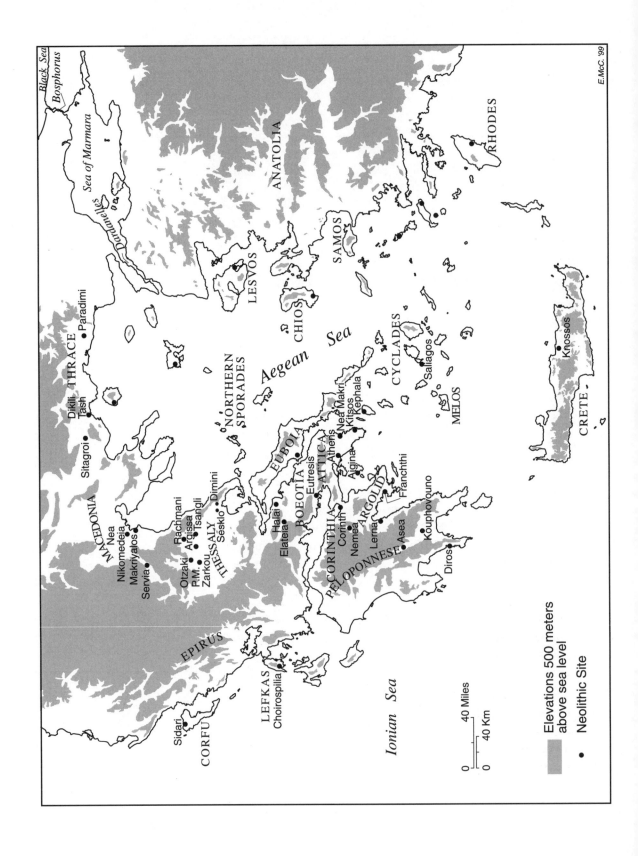

Black Sea

Bosphorus

Sea of Marmara

Dardanelles

THRACE

Paradimi

Dikili
Tash

Sitagroi

MACEDONIA

Nea
Nikomedeia

Makriyalos

Servia

Otzaki
P.M.
Zarkou

Rachmani

Argissa
Tsangli

THESSALY

Sesklo

Dimini

ANATOLIA

LESVOS

CHIOS

SAMOS

Aegean   Sea

NORTHERN
SPORADES

EUBOIA

Halai

Elatela

BOEOTIA

Eutresis

ATTICA

Athens

Nea Makri

Kitsos

Kephala

Aigina

PECORINTHIA

Corinth

Nemea

Lerna

ARGOLID

Franchthi

PELOPONNESE

Asea

Kouphovouno

Diros

EPIRUS

LEFKAS

Choirospilia

CORFU

Sidari

Ionian   Sea

CYCLADES

Saliagos

MELOS

RHODES

CRETE

Knossos

E.McC. '99

40 Miles

40 Km

Elevations 500 meters
above sea level

•   Neolithic Site

been used for close to 10,000 years to create entirely new species of plants and animals that depend on human intervention to survive.

Domesticated sheep and cattle differ significantly from their wild progenitors in ways, such as size, that are obvious to the eye. Domesticated plants differ from their wild forms in the same way, and few people today recognize the connection between major food crops like wheat and maize and the simple grasses that gave rise to them. The genetic differences are great enough to warrant the designation of the new species of domesticated plants and animals as *artificial* productions, a view that entirely supports the traditional designation of the Neolithic as a distinct economic epoch characterized by the production of food. The prehistorian V. Gordon Childe argued that the Neolithic Revolution, as he called it, was of the same order and importance to human history as the Urban Revolution in the fourth millennium B.C. and the Industrial Revolution in the eighteenth century because of the profound social and cultural transformations that were entrained in the economic process of domestication and full-scale farming. In the sense that "revolution" means "profound change" and does not imply anything about the direction or tempo of the change involved, we agree with this view.

In Greece the Neolithic began with the appearance on many sites of fully domesticated species of wheat, barley, beans, and lentils, along with animals such as sheep, goat, and pigs (see Figure 3.1). These changes in flora and fauna were accompanied by many technological advances as well. The principal changes went far beyond the use of polished stone axes and querns and included stone and adobe brick architecture, permanently inhabited villages with populations in the hundreds, pottery, ceramic sculptures, woolen textiles, and decorative arts in many materials (see Figure 3.2). The beginning of the Neolithic in Greece is marked by a fundamental revolution of the economic mode of life and a dazzling burst of innovation in the sphere of material culture. The appearance of farming villages in Greece was indeed

3.1 *Opposite.* The locations of the principal excavated Neolithic sites. The actual number of sites is much larger. In the eastern portion of Thessaly alone there are nearly 400 documented sites in an area of roughly 1,000 square kilometers with Argissa at the center. Most are on the eastern half of the mainland, becoming much less frequent to the north, west, and south into the Cyclades islands.

a profound revolution in human history and brought into existence a way of life that has remained the basis of European society to the present day.

Archaeologists agree that the first steps toward settled village life and agriculture in this part of the world took place in the Near East, not in Greece. For this purpose, the Near East encompasses a vast geographic area that includes a large part of eastern Turkey and all of the modern countries of Syria, Iraq, Lebanon, Jordan, Israel, and parts of Iran. It is in this geographic area that the wild ancestors of today's domesticated plants and animals had their natural range, and here too are found the oldest traces of permanent villages based on the new agricultural economy.

Tracing the entire process responsible for the Neolithic revolution in the Near East would take us too far afield, but perhaps it is sufficient to note that the process was already under way when the Pleistocene gave way to the Holocene. By 10,000 B.P. permanent villages existed in the Levant and the hill country of northern Iraq, and the plant remains found with the querns used to process them testify to the fact that cultivation was under way. By 8000 B.P. the entire Near Eastern region was filled with farming villages exhibiting the full panoply of Neolithic material culture. This much has been established by intensive archaeological research over the past fifty years.

The explanation for this revolution is more controversial, with theories that range from an environmental push brought about by climate change, to the pressure on food resources brought about by a grow-

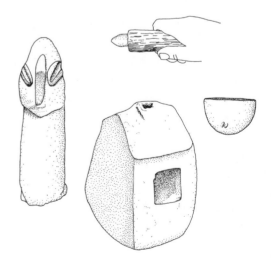

3.2   The Neolithic period saw the introduction of many new features, including pottery, polished hard stone axes (*top right*), often hafted with wooden or antler handles, substantial domestic architecture (house model at *bottom right*), and a large variety of terra-cotta and stone anthropomorphic figurines.

ing population, to hypotheses that demographic movements, growing trade and commerce, or even demand for sacrificial animals for religious practices caused a gradual drift into farming. No one theory has succeeded in winning the day, and the origin of the Neolithic in a general sense remains one of the most interesting problems in archaeology. Our view is that it is better to avoid this larger question here and to concentrate on a smaller question. How did the Neolithic begin in our small region, which is thought to lie outside the core area of Neolithic origins?

THE ORIGINS OF THE GREEK NEOLITHIC

Theories to explain the transition from foraging to farming in Greece have had their fads and fashions much like the theories connected with the Neanderthals. Early in the twentieth century the proximity of Greece to the Near East encouraged archaeologists to look to "diffusion," either cultural (movement of artifacts and ideas) or demic (movement of people), as an explanation. This line of thinking was strongly supported by the theoretical work of V. Gordon Childe, an Australian archaeologist at the University of Edinburgh, who demonstrated the primary nature of Near Eastern and Egyptian moves toward agriculture and the fundamental similarity of the Neolithic cultures that appeared in neighboring geographic regions such as Greece.

The hypothesis of diffusion from the Near East to explain the Greek Neolithic was well established in the literature for most of the period from the 1920s to the 1970s until a new theoretical movement, sometimes dubbed "indigenism" or "independent invention," began to gain ground. For supporters of these views there was no need to invoke diffusion at all. They argued that foragers everywhere were familiar with the qualities of plants and animals in their environment and that farming would emerge more or less spontaneously in every region where the conditions were right. Because of climate change or demographic pressure, foragers would experiment with native plants and animals in order to increase food supplies, and these experiments resulted in the gradual emergence of the full farming economy. Any similarities in material culture among neighboring farmers could be explained entirely by small-scale exchanges of pottery or textiles that would foster similar developments in the receiving culture by a process called stimulus diffusion.

If the older view of demic and cultural diffusion of farming helped explain the appearance of the Neolithic in regions adjacent to the Near East, the new theories of independent invention went a long way toward explaining the demonstrably independent appearance of farming in Mesoamerica, sub-Saharan Africa, China, and Southeast Asia. Since the 1980s, however, the indigenist hypothesis has been rejected as an explanation for the Greek Neolithic and replaced by another theory based on diffusion. How this change came about requires some explaining.

The Evidence for Diffusion

Scientists agree that the plant and animal species that formed the core of the Greek Neolithic economy originated in the Near East. Carbonized plant remains and animal bones from excavations such as Franchthi Cave permit the precise identification of the varieties that were present at early sites. The earliest Neolithic farmers in Greece utilized domesticated forms of grain and animals, all with solid pedigrees from Southwest Asia (see Figure 3.3). There was experimentation with wild barley and lentils at Mesolithic Franchthi Cave, but these experiments did not lead to domestication. There were also no wild stocks of goats or sheep on the Greek peninsula, and thus the domestic forms that appeared at the beginning of the Neolithic were also brought from the Near East where the wild forms had their natural range (see Figure 3.4).

The Neolithic at Franchthi began abruptly with fully domesticated plants species very different from the Mesolithic varieties and with precisely the same species of domesticated plants and animals as were found in earlier sites in the Near East.

Settlement patterns support a modified hypothesis of agricultural origins by diffusion. In the 1970s the lack of excavations and surveys directed toward the discovery of Palaeolithic and Mesolithic sites left the field open to speculation. Some postulated that if Greece had had a large indigenous population in the run-up to the Neolithic, migrating Near Eastern farmers would have had difficulty making inroads in a land already occupied by a settled native population with their own program of food production. New regional surveys conducted since then have at last given us reliable figures for determining the Old Stone Age settlement pattern on the eve of the Neolithic.

We searched for sites of the Late Palaeolithic and Mesolithic in Thessaly, for example, and found that this region, which was the center of Neolithic civilization from approximately 9000 B.P. on, had no detectable population in the millennia preceding the Neolithic era. Only Theopetra Cave, about an hour's drive to the west of Larisa, shows any sign of Mesolithic occupation, and as a consequence it stands out by its very rarity. Surveys in Macedonia, Thrace, and parts of the Peloponnese have shown a similar lack of pre-Neolithic populations. Only in the Argolid and western Epirus/Corfu was any evidence found for Mesolithic people; but, as we have already seen, these people were themselves no more "indigenous" than the Neolithic peoples who succeeded them. The Mesolithic marks the first wave of demic diffusion from the Near East.

Archaeological evidence from the period of transition from the Mesolithic to the Neolithic is necessary if the discussion of diffusion is to make progress, and in Greece the transition from the Palaeolithic

3.3 Wheat and barley were introduced from the Near East at the beginning of the Neolithic. The domesticated forms of these grasses have been part of the human food chain for 10,000 years. As this book was being written, wheat was the first food plant to be successfully cultivated in space aboard the NASA space shuttle.

3.4 Sheep (*left*) and goats (*right*) were also introduced at the beginning of the Neolithic. At first they were used to convert coarse native vegetation and crop stubble into meat, but there is evidence that they were increasingly exploited for wool and hair to weave textiles and for milk to make cheese and yogurt.

to the Mesolithic and the Neolithic can be followed at only one excavated and dated site. Again Franchthi Cave provides a key sequence of evidence.

We have already observed that the Palaeolithic and the Mesolithic are separated by a hiatus or break in the stratigraphic record, from which we conclude that the resumption of occupation in the Mesolithic represented the arrival of new inhabitants at the site. The transition from the Mesolithic to the Neolithic appears uninterrupted, but the changeover from Mesolithic to Neolithic takes place in about 30 centimeters of the same archaeological stratum with abrupt and far-reaching cultural and economic changes.

Within the cave itself, the earliest Neolithic deposits produced bones of domesticated sheep and goats, which replaced the deer and pig of the Mesolithic, and domesticated wheat and barley, which replaced wild barley and lentils as the main plant foods. Pottery appears to have been present from the beginning of the Neolithic, already technically developed and sophisticated. Polished stone axes were added to the repertoire along with small clay and stone figurines and ornaments.

On the shore directly outside the mouth of the cave the transition is even more dramatic. Founded directly on sterile soil is a small village (now partly submerged by the rising sea) of large rectangular buildings with stone foundations and adobe brick or rammed clay walls topped with beams and thatch. Rich finds of a Neolithic type are found in these buildings and throughout the site, as are the graves of children and adults, some with grave goods. Particularly noteworthy is the grave, in the cave, of a small infant in a stone-lined pit; the infant was accompanied by a clay pot split down the middle (ritually "killed") and a finely worked bowl of marble imported from the Cycladic islands. This grave is evidence of the growing complexity of Neolithic life. The rich finds suggest the high status of the child, and the marble bowl is evidence of trade and craft specialization.

Although some of the older Mesolithic stone-working techniques found expression in the later Neolithic technology, a fact that suggests some contact took place between the two populations, the evidence suggests that village farmers arrived with a fully developed Neolithic economy. The possibility that these settlers arrived at Franchthi from elsewhere in Greece must be considered, but at least two sites give clear evidence that they migrated by sea, almost certainly after crossings of some considerable length. These sites are Sidari (on Corfu) and Knossos (on Crete). At Knossos, a site otherwise famous for the Palace of Minos, the center of the Bronze Age Minoan civilization, excavation below the palace in the 1960s by the British archaeologist John Evans brought to light a deeply stratified deposit of Neolithic remains reaching back to nearly 9000 B.P. (the same time as the earliest Neolithic sites in the rest of Greece). Here too the Neolithic economy arrived on the island as a complete package with stone architecture, pottery, and domesticated species of plants and animals. When one considers that the island was isolated by open sea throughout the Pleistocene and had no human inhabitants in the Palaeolithic, the only possible conclusion is that the first settlers at Knossos reached the island of Crete by boat. There is no question here of the independent invention of agriculture. There were no natives, and we can confidently conclude that Neolithic Knossos was founded by seafaring colonists. That they came from the Near East (in a broad sense) is attested by the domesticated wheat and barley and sheep, goats, and cattle. None of these domesticates has a wild ancestor on Crete.

The site of Sidari on Corfu far to the west in the Ionian Sea has a similar history. We have already described the Mesolithic shell midden that was excavated on the north coast of Corfu by Augustus Sordinas, but at Sidari an Early Neolithic layer overlays the earlier Mesolithic shell midden. The Neolithic layer contains simple pottery and the bones of domesticated animals, none of which have antecedents in the underlying Mesolithic midden. The relationship between the two layers is unclear, but the boundary between them is visible today as a clear and distinct line, which suggests that there was an abrupt discontinuity between the two periods. Whether Sidari was settled by one migration or two, its settlers were undoubtedly seafaring migrants because the island was cut off from the mainland by the rising sea at the end of the Pleistocene before the site was first inhabited. No doubt the further exploration of the Cycladic and other large Aegean islands will turn up additional Mesolithic sites like Sidari (the still poorly known site of Maroula on the Cycladic island of Kythnos may be one).

The Beginnings of Neolithic Life

The facts are convincing on the question of how the Neolithic got to Greece. It arrived as the result of the migration of humans (demic diffusion) beginning around 9000 B.P. The pattern of settlement, which is focused on the larger islands and coastal areas of Greece and other Mediterranean lands, supports the hypothesis of demic diffusion by sea. This diffusion may have begun at the beginning of the Mesolithic period, some one or two millennia earlier, and it certainly continued for some time. The success of settlements such as Knossos on Crete would have required the continued additions of humans, seeds, and animal stocks to make up losses attributable to crop failure and disease. Despite our certainty about the diffusion, however, we still do not know where the colonists came from or why they undertook such a difficult and dangerous migration.

Partial answers are possible for both questions. In recent decades archaeologists have largely accepted a model from biology to help explain the general process of animal and, by analogy, human dispersals. This model is called the Wave of Advance, and it can be combined effectively with the demic diffusion hypothesis we are working with here.

The Wave of Advance model has two major postulates: that the population growth that accompanies the shift to farming will be fast at first but will eventually level off, and that populations will expand at their margins at a more or less constant rate through a series of small-scale and essentially random movements. Population near the center will, by contrast, be relatively stable, and growth occurs only on the margins. It is the population growth on the frontier that causes the more or less steady wave-of-advance effect.

Assuming as a working hypothesis that farming first emerged in the Near East and that farming triggered population growth (a critical assumption, supported by existing data), we can assert that the Wave of Advance moved outward from the core to the periphery of the Near East—that is, to Greece—at a rate of about one kilometer every generation. The similar house forms (stone foundations with mud-brick walls), pottery (red and white decorations), figurines (reclining, sitting, and standing females with abstract features), and other aspects of material culture in Greece and Anatolia (modern Turkey) all point to Asia Minor as a proximal source of Neolithic farmers. The resemblances between the cultures of the Anatolian plateau and Thessaly are striking (see Figure 3.5).

But why would whole families pack up and risk their lives and fortunes in the sea crossing from Asian shores to the Greek islands and the mainland? There were no charts or maps, no safeguards, and no certainty of success in a new territory, even if they survived the voyage. And yet we know that they did it, and the island settlement of Knossos shows that they brought their farm animals and seed crops as well. What was it like, we wonder, to cross to Crete on a small Neolithic boat (perhaps no more than a dugout or a small raft of logs) with frightened sheep and cows, crazed billy goats, and seasick pigs?

Neolithic farmers had very simple technology. They broke the soil with digging sticks and cultivated and harvested their crops of wheat and barley with stone hoes and flint sickles. Sheep, cattle, and pigs could forage on the hillsides and root through crop stubble and village refuse heaps. Any cropland had to be cleaned of trees and brush with fire and polished stone axes. This limited technology encouraged the early farmers to settle close to springs, streams, and rivers where a steady supply of water ensured the survival of small crops in tiny fields and gardens. In river floodplains, floodwater in winter and spring suppressed the growth of trees and brought nutrients to the previous year's fields.

Because of the limited scope and special requirements of Neolithic farming, the best conditions were hard to find. Once the optimal sites were occupied by other farmers, newcomers had to search farther afield. For unknown reasons, farming populations tend to grow faster than those of hunter-gatherers or foragers, and the population growth encouraged farmers in their search for prime agricultural land.

In Greece, the Neolithic farmers settled in all parts of the country, although at first they established themselves in a few regions and on the bigger islands of Corfu, Crete, and Rhodes. On the mainland, Thessaly was the center of Neolithic civilization for as long as a thousand years, primarily because of the nearby Peneios River. It flows through an enclosed basin formed by the gradual subsidence of its rocky foundation. The course of the river has remained fixed from the high

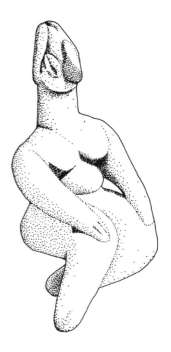

3.5 A Neolithic terra-cotta anthropomorphic figurine of the seated type similar to examples found in contemporary sites on the central Anatolia plateau (e.g., Çatal Höyük and Hacılar). The similarity of such figurines in Anatolia and the Near East may imply a continuity of cult (if these are religious representations).

Pindos Mountains to the sea, where it passes through the famous Vale of Tempe. Melting winter snows flooded the river in the spring and summer, enriching the plain with mud and silt and soaking all the soils with water that would support crops the year round. Like a small Nile River, the Peneios attracted farmers to its banks, and today their settlements dot the Peneios valley like anthills in the Serengeti Plain of Tanzania.

NEOLITHIC CIVILIZATION

There are few large alluvial plains in Greece, and the landscape around Larisa in Thessaly reminds one of the landscape of Kansas or perhaps the plains of the Danube Basin in Hungary.

As one follows the main road north from Athens toward Thessaloniki and enters the Thessalian plain, the landscape opens up with the peaks of Mounts Pelion, Ossa, and Olympus visible on the skyline. At first the rolling plain appears featureless, but then one notices here and there low mounds that break the monotony. In some areas, particularly around the city of Larisa, these mounds are quite numerous. All of them are the sites of Neolithic villages, the remains of the first great civilization on European soil. The mounds consist of clay, stone tools, pottery, and other debris derived from the decayed building materials left by more than a hundred generations of people. These mounds are called "tells" by archaeologists (in Greek, *magoules*).

The Thessalian plain has two great parts, the eastern section around Larisa and a western section centered on Trikala. The Neolithic *magoules* in the eastern part of the plain have been inventoried by a Greek team, which recorded more than 350 surviving *magoules*, a testament to the large and successful Neolithic culture in this area. Excavation began early there, in the 1890s by the Greek archaeologist Christos Tsountas, and since the 1950s by teams led by archaeologists Demetrios Theocharis, Vladimir Milojcic, Georgios Hourmouziadis, and Konstantine Gallis.

The outlines of Neolithic civilization can be reconstructed from the artifacts and other data recovered from excavated *magoules*. Neolithic civilization persisted for some 4,000 years, from 9000 B.P. to 5000 B.P., and is divided by archaeologists into four phases, Early, Middle, Late, and Final Neolithic, which for convenience can be considered as lasting between 500 and 1,000 years each. Throughout this long period the simple village, with 100 to 400 inhabitants living in closely spaced houses, was the central feature of the culture. Only toward the end of the period did the inhabitants begin to experiment with metals such as silver, gold, and copper. For most of the period, their simple technology was based on tools of stone. But unlike the preceding phases of the Stone Age, the Neolithic was a time of great innovation in material culture and probably in other areas as well, such as religion.

Clay models found at the sites reveal that Neolithic houses were probably constructed of mud bricks (adobe) on stone foundations. Thatched roofs appear to have been covered with thick layers of clay that were sometimes painted bright colors. The roofs were pitched and equipped with smoke holes, and doors and windows were outlined with brightly painted red and white decorations. Some models appear to portray two-story structures (corroborated with archaeological finds). At least one model found buried under the wall of a real house contains numerous anthropomorphic and zoomorphic forms. It is thought to be a "foundation deposit," a kind of good-luck offering placed there when the house was being constructed. The other models may have had such uses.

If the actual village houses looked anything like the house models, they must have presented a colorful, even vibrant, picture: a tightly packed village of white houses with bright red painted decorations sitting amidst fields of green grass, or perhaps in the gold of ripening wheat in the brilliant sun of early summer (see Figure 3.6). The effect may not have been unlike that still to be seen in some traditional

3.6   An impression of what a Neolithic Greek village may have looked like. Houses were built of adobe brick on stone foundations with thatched roofs. House models suggest that doors, windows, smoke holes, and painted plaster decoration on exterior walls were common features of Neolithic houses.

Greek villages today, although in the Neolithic, clouds of dust raised by herds of sheep and goats moving through the little lanes, the pall of smoke from family hearths, and the stench of the slops on the middens in the streets and between the houses would have been prevalent.

Excavation has recovered a wealth of detail connected with daily life in Neolithic times. Excavations within the house ruins recovered typical tools, including polished stone axes, flint sickles, clay spindle whorls used to spin yarn, bone tools such as awls, and abundant remains of food (see Figure 3.7). The principal food remains are preserved by carbonization in fires, either cooking fires or accidental fires that destroyed a structure; they include wheat, barley, peas and other

3.7 Reconstructions of Neolithic houses are based on the well-preserved stone foundations at sites such as Sesklo and Dimini. They were almost always rectangular in outline but varied considerably in size from no more than about two meters on a side to 25 meters in length. The full range of functions is not known. Some buildings may have been shrines or had public uses.

legumes, and a wide variety of fruits and nuts. Animal bones include those of sheep, goats, cattle, and pigs. Also found are figurines of various materials and some stone or shell ornaments. Rough stone querns were used to grind plant foods, and a few odds and ends, such as the "computers" discussed below, defy classification. Such materials would not have been out of place in simple farmsteads right into the eighteenth and nineteenth centuries throughout the Balkans. All that is missing are wooden shelves, a few sticks of furniture, and the colorful woolen textiles that probably covered them.

Stone axes were among the most important tools in the Neolithic, and the manufacture of these implements by polishing hard, green, igneous stones on a rough quern is the feature that originally gave the Neolithic its name. The axes were mounted in antler sockets that were set in wooden handles to absorb shock. These axes were very effective for felling trees and working wood (to make boats and houses). Danish archaeologists in the 1950s demonstrated their effectiveness by using actual Neolithic axes to chop down trees. They estimated that Neolithic farmers could have cleared an acre of forest in a matter of hours.

Simple pointed tools of bone and antler resemble tools used today in some parts of Greece to make baskets. Some of the painted pottery designs resemble basketry, and we imagine a rich array of baskets once existed. Other tools were used to process foods. The simple querns, mortars, and pestles were employed to crush hard grains before cooking, to break the shells of nuts, and to pulp berries and powder herbs. They were probably also used to crush minerals, plants, and insects for use as coloring agents for textiles and pottery.

A variety of bone and clay tools were used in weaving. Spindle whorls are conical in shape with a vertical perforation. Mounted on a stick, they were used as weights to help turn the stick and collect yarn as it was spun from a bunch of wool or hair held in the fork of another stick. The ability to weave wool from sheep and hair from goats made these animals more valuable for this commodity than for their meat. Although the textiles themselves have not survived, the presence of the whorls, which have no other known use, are indication enough of the craft. We can imagine the textiles in a range of hues, including red, brown, yellow, and blue, supplied by natural dyes made from acorns and other plants. The designs are thought to be similar to those found on the pottery, or indeed in present-day Anatolian flat woven carpets such as kilims: triangles, diamonds, and chevrons. Houses throughout the eastern Mediterranean world in our own time are often filled with such textiles, and the pleasing colorful effect would have greatly enhanced the otherwise technically simple Neolithic houses.

Neolithic lives were enriched with art in the form of varied and beautifully executed painted pots and a stunning array of human and animal figurines in clay and stone. The thousands of specimens are evidence of the inventiveness of their creators. Nearly every village seems to have had its own style of painted pot, and shapes and decorative schemes appear in bewildering plentitude. But there is a certain unity evident in the pottery. All of the pottery was handmade and fired in simple pits or small kilns similar to bread ovens (see Figure 3.8).

The colors were achieved with pigments from minerals such as ochre and copper ore, and colored clays contributed white and tan tones. With these simple materials the potter created first-rate ceramics with thin walls and bright colors, which were durable and no doubt serviceable as well. They are usually decorated with a dark figure on a light ground, usually red on white, and an abundance of abstract, geometric designs reminiscent of textile decoration.

Neolithic pottery is decorated with repetitive patterns of squares, nets, and curved triangles (or "flame" patterns). Human and animal forms appear only in the figurines, which demonstrate the Neolithic mastery of animate forms and artistic skill. We must assume that the abstract designs on the painted pottery were the result of deliberate choice (see Figure 3.9). Why they produced so much delicate, beautifully painted pottery with only a limited repertoire of designs is a genuine puzzle for archaeologists. K. D. Vitelli of Indiana University has noted that very little of the highest-quality pottery was used for storage or cooking. Many of the most carefully made pots are small bowls or cups that cannot be easily covered to store goods. We know that more coarsely made undecorated pots were used for cooking, at least in the later phases of the Neolithic, because these have traces of burning on their bottoms or food residues inside. But the finely decorated pots obviously served another purpose; perhaps they were used for

3.8   Neolithic pottery in Thessaly was handmade and fired under carefully controlled conditions. It is of very high technical quality. Decorations were usually abstract designs painted in red on an off-white background.

display in the house as an indication of status, much as a service of fine antique china might be displayed today.

This pottery may have been handmade and fired in crude pits and bread ovens, but it is not technologically primitive. The pots were hard-fired, often at temperatures high enough to fuse the metallic pigments and clay slips on the surface and form a shiny durable "glaze." The two-tone effects of the painted pottery often required two or more separate firings and a precise experimental knowledge of clays, pigments, and fuels. Modern experimenters have succeeded in duplicating Neolithic pottery, but only after years of painstaking study, many failures, and careful attention to detail. It is not an easy craft, and the high success rate of Neolithic potters is testimony to their professional craftsmanship. Each village seems to have had its own production of these pots (K. D. Vitelli believes it was a craft pursued primarily by women in individual households). The variety of design found from village to village is notable. Their adherence to the same basic elements of design (such as geometric patterns) is evidence, however, of some larger unifying principle that we have yet to grasp: one of the mysteries of Neolithic civilization (see Figure 3.10).

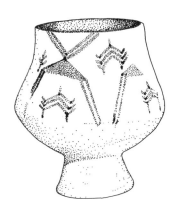

3.9 Neolithic pottery varied regionally beginning about 7500 B.P. In the Peloponnese, for instance, the pottery was decorated in a reddish brown paint on a buff-colored ground. This so-called Urfirnis (early glazed) ware has a lustrous metallic finish achieved by a method not yet fully understood. Although the forms and decorations are similar to those seen in Thessaly at the same time, pottery from the two regions is easily distinguished by techniques of firing and other details.

3.10 Later Neolithic pottery is notable for its use of polychrome decoration in red or black on a light-colored background and the wider use of handles and spiral design motifs.

Another mystery of the Greek Neolithic is the meaning of the immense variety of figures in clay and stone that have tantalized, amazed, and puzzled a generation of archaeologists. Small figurines of humans and animals have been found around the world, some made as early as 30,000 years ago (in western Europe), and more or less continuously from then on. The figurines manufactured by the ancient Egyptians are plentiful enough today to fill whole museums, and they were common in cultures as different as classical Greece and ancient China. Even in modern homes many a mantelpiece displays porcelain figurines, and children's bedrooms have them in abundance in the form of Barbie dolls and "action figures."

Yet archaeologists can agree on only one point concerning the ancient figurines: that we do not know what they meant to the people who made them. Neolithic figurines come in a bewildering array of sizes and shapes, and their decorative details are just as varied. Can they have anything in common? Many are of nude females; far fewer are of male and animal forms. This can be a little misleading, however, because many figurines have no certain indication of gender, although they may resemble the female form (see Figure 3.11).

Another curious feature is the abstraction of the face, which is often shown with cowrie-shell eyes and less often with ears, nose, or mouth (a cowrie is a marine mollusk). All of them have exaggerated physical features such as long cylindrical necks, pointed heads, large buttocks, and vestigial hands or feet (sometimes these are left out altogether) (see Figure 3.12). In short, they are not realistic or naturalistic portrayals of humans, but only general humanoid forms. Finally, most figurines are standing or sitting individuals; the lack of groups or of the depiction of activity (such as craftwork, farming, or dancing) is noticeable. Perhaps this abstraction and simplification of form is the unifying principle behind the figurines, as it is for the pottery (see Figure 3.13).

White marble, plain clay, and clay painted with red or brown abstract designs are the principal media used in the manufacture of figurines. The pure abstraction of the crosslike or violin-shaped marble

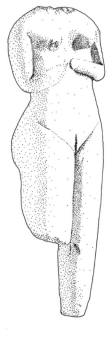

3.11 A terra-cotta female figurine from Lerna in the Argolid.

3.12　A terra-cotta female(?) figurine from Thessaly in the pose most widely depicted in Neolithic figurines.

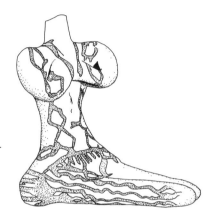

3.13　A terra-cotta female figurine from Franchthi Cave with painted decoration that may be intended to show textiles or body decoration of some kind. Neolithic figurines are frequently missing heads or other parts and may sometimes have been deliberately broken in what is sometimes called the "ritual killing" of artifacts.

figures changes in time to the startling realism of heads with detailed and recognizable features, painted red, and resembling the face of a newborn child. In this great range of expression, tightly bound as it is within a narrow cordon of convention, we have a recognizable pattern of meaning, the key to which has been lost forever. The findspots of figurines tell us nothing about their function. They are found everywhere in Neolithic villages, even in the refuse pits. The great number of figurines, however, is signal evidence of their importance.

The absence of evidence that specific beliefs were attached to these figurines, or even that they had any particular use, has opened up the field to sometimes wild speculation. Figurines may appear special, and the natural impulse is to consider them idols of some sort representing the gods and goddesses of these ancient people. But figurines need not automatically have a religious use. Let us remember the role of dolls in our own culture; and Chinese doctors in past centuries used figurines to indicate to female patients the location of their problems in order to honor their modesty.

Figurines can have many uses that range from the mostly misunderstood "voodoo" dolls of Caribbean religion to the purely aesthetic creations of artists today. The use of figurines can change over time: an ancient Roman figurine sitting in a modern museum display case has a different meaning for those who created it and those who view it today. More than twice as much time separates the earliest Greek Neolithic from the latest phase of the same culture (4,000 years) than separates our time from the Roman period. Finally, context matters absolutely in any interpretation. A plastic figurine of a Christian saint on the dashboard of a car invokes the saint's protection, but what would future archaeologists make of the same figurine found in a landfill or dump?

Such niceties of interpretation have not deterred archaeologists from venturing to interpret Neolithic figurines, and almost everyone seems to think that they have something to do with religious belief, like the figurines of later pagan religions of the Bronze Age in the Near East and in the classical Greco-Roman world. Although this is a reasonable assumption for some of the figurines, it is unlikely to be the whole story. First, we are able to interpret the meanings of figurines in the later periods from textual accounts of religious practice; the lack of Neolithic writing makes this impossible for that earlier period. Second, the great variety of figurines suggests that they do not represent a single set of clearly recognizable deities; and last, the contexts in which they are found tell us little or nothing about what the ancients thought of them.

Figurines from Thessalian Neolithic sites have been found in house deposits, dumps, middens, pits, and virtually everywhere within a site, suggesting that they were as readily discarded as they were easy to make. No recognizable temples or shrines have been identified, and even the meaning of figurines found in a special deposit, such as the house model buried under a floor, remains ambiguous. Are they figures of deities, or do they represent the worshipers? Are they priests and priestesses or the ghosts of departed ancestors? How would one tell them apart without an identifying label?

Burials are also connected with prehistoric belief, ritual and ceremonial. Burials in the Neolithic were sometimes simple interments, often beneath the floors of houses, but cremation was also practiced, and entire fields of pots containing the partly burned remains of humans are known from sites late in the Neolithic period. The fact of burial and the variety of methods employed may reflect spiritual belief and the earthly status of the dead when they were alive and suggest that their beliefs were highly developed and complex. The buried bodies are rarely accompanied by grave goods, although sometimes a few simple tools have been found in the pit; for example, a woman at Franchthi Cave was buried with a kit of bone points and obsidian blades, suggesting that she had been a basket weaver. More often a pot or two, sometimes ritually "killed" by breaking it into pieces, was placed in the grave. The body was usually folded into the fetal position, in some cases only after the bones had been "defleshed" by exposure for a period of days or weeks. Cremations were more elaborate. After being burned, the remains were carefully packed into fine pots, which in turn were buried in pits. Whole cemeteries of cremated remains have been uncovered.

Some artifacts have so far defied analysis, such as "seals" and small rectangular objects dubbed "computers" by puzzled archaeologists. Seals are usually made of stone (often pierced for suspension on a cord) and carved with geometric patterns common in weavings today and commonly referred to as "sun" or "star" patterns. Archaeologists have called them seals because they might have been used to impress designs in soft clay or to stamp designs in color on wood, clothing, or skin. But frankly, we have no idea what people did with them.

The "computers" get their nickname from the variety of dots and signs that cover the surface, which resemble some kind of quantitative computation or primitive writing or recording system. Found only in recent years and in very small numbers, they have not yet been studied or appeared in print, but they raise the tantalizing possibility that the Neolithic Thessalians had a simple notational system, a key ingredient in the development and advancement of complex society or civilization (see Figure 3.14).

Early students of the Neolithic civilization of Thessaly regarded it

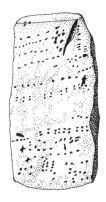
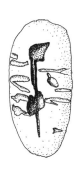

3.14 Neolithic "computers." These small terra-cotta objects from Sesklo have signs incised on the surface that may be notations of some kind.

as rather simple in social terms, consisting of egalitarian societies of simple farmer folk, isolated, conservative, focused on subsistence agriculture and survival, and persisting with little change for centuries or even millennia. Some popular writings depict these farmer folk as living in a "golden age" without the corruption of luxury or the evils of social inequality and war. But this view is completely unsupported by the evidence, however attractive it might be.

The presence of Melian obsidian, exotic stone ornaments and axes, and other materials that must have been traded from one place to another is evidence of a sophisticated economy. Some Neolithic trade was long distance. Shell ornaments (arm bands, rings, bangles) made from the spiny Mediterranean oyster, *Spondylus gaederopus*, have been found in European Neolithic contexts as far north as Poland, and large honey-colored flint blades in Greece may have been procured from as far away as Bulgaria or Romania. The regional variation in pottery styles, when it is coupled with the data on trade and other regional craft activity, suggests that economic activity grew and became ever more complex. This economic complexity is paralleled by evidence of social complexity. Village buildings, for instance, varied in size; presumably some were used for special functions or were constructed to meet the specific requirements of individuals and families. Mortuary practice is also evidence of social complexity: some individuals, including women and children, received careful interment within the settlement while adult males were evidently disposed of elsewhere. Not all burials were accompanied by grave goods, and the different burial practices (interment and cremation) may have reflected something like social status.

The general structure of Neolithic life, which was based in small, tightly clustered villages, with an economy firmly grounded in agriculture and animal husbandry, was not unlike rural life in Greece through the millennia to the present day. The Neolithic period, then, introduced and established a way of life that would support, shape, and sometimes constrain all later developments. We should always bear in mind that the glamorous monuments of the classical period in Greece, both physical (as represented by the Parthenon) and intellectual (science, philosophy, and drama) were achieved by people who lived in villages and small towns and were supported by an agricultural economy that was perfected after millennia of trial and error by the Neolithic farmers.

One other Neolithic artifact can be viewed from virtually anyplace in Greece: the landscape. It is to a large extent the work of Neolithic farmers over a period of nearly 4,000 years. The first migrants found a land forested with deciduous oaks, beech, ash, pine, and other species. These trees held a thick cover of soil on many hills. Rivers and streams incised their beds with water, and lakes provided a rich habitat for wildfowl, fish, and amphibians. Records of ancient pollen show that the first farmers had little effect on the forest cover of Greece for the first thousand years or so, but beginning around 5000 B.P. the pollen from the trees began to decline, and the pollen of shrubby species tolerant of dry conditions such as scrub oak, juniper, and sage increased. The process of forest clearing recorded by the pollen record accelerated after 4500 B.P. and was at times catastrophic.

When a forest is cleared and the roots no longer anchor the soil, it may begin to erode. The resulting surfaces of bare rock reflect more sunlight into space in a well-known process that inhibits rainfall and leads to the loss of even more trees. Such a cycle results in an arid landscape dominated by low woody shrubs that require less water and soil.

By 4000 B.P. soil erosion caused by deforestation had occurred in many parts of Greece. Although the process of desertification can in part be attributed to the gradual drying of the climate, there is strong evidence that humans accelerated the process. Desertification created a landscape of rocky slopes covered with a thin chaparral, maquis (scrubby underbrush), and garigue (more open scrubland with low trees and bunchgrasses). Evergreen oak, heather, and herbs such as oregano and thyme, bare, sun-drenched islands, and dry stream beds constitute the landscape one sees in much of Greece today.

Finally, archaeologists, historians, folklorists, philologists, and linguists have long sought to determine when the direct ancestors of the Greek-speaking inhabitants of the Balkan peninsula first made their appearance. Opinions differ widely. Some scholars place their origin no earlier than the early Iron Age (some 2,700 years ago), while others see the Greek entrance to the Balkan scene in the Late Bronze Age (3,500 years ago), at the beginning of the Middle Bronze Age (4,300 years ago), or even at the beginning of the Neolithic period (8,800 years ago). This question is really only of academic interest, but emotions sometimes run high on the subject. Modern Greeks are naturally interested in knowing when their ancestors established themselves in the fabled motherland of Hellas. The answer to the question has sometimes had political overtones as well: today, for example, there is strife over lands now occupied by persons of other ethnic groups that were peopled by Greeks in the distant past.

Anyone considering this question, however, would be well advised to ponder the seeming continuity in the fabric of Greek economic and social life from the Neolithic period onward. There are certainly some discontinuities and dislocations in the archaeological record, some of which we discuss in later chapters, but the *texture*, if we can call it that, of village farming life, of social activity, of artistic expression, even of social status and architectural form, was already established before 5000 B.C.

It seems to us an inevitable conclusion that Greek life as we know it from the annals of history began in the humble Neolithic village of Thessaly and the Peloponnese. To say that little has changed in Greek village life from the Neolithic to early industrial times is a cliché and an oversimplification, of course, and while it may be true that mud-brick houses, agricultural rhythms, and simple tools and pots have similarities across the centuries, culture has also changed, as it is expressed in language, custom, kinship, the arts, religion, and social structure. But patterns of life do persist for centuries, and in the absence of evidence of great rifts in this fabric we have no reason to suppose that a profound change in ethnicity, however this may be defined, has occurred. Neolithic civilization stands as the first true Greek civilization, indeed the first recorded European civilization, and for this reason the few precious finds recovered from archaeological excavations in the Thessalian tells have special significance for the world.

CHAPTER FOUR

THE BRONZE AGE

"Savage Virtues and Barbarous Grandeur"

Speaking of his visit to the Highlands of Scotland in the eighteenth century, Dr. Johnson noted the gradual disappearance of traditional ways and remarked that "a longer journey than to the Highlands must be taken by him whose curiosity pants for savage virtues and barbarous grandeur." An age of savage virtues and barbarous grandeur strikes us as a fit description of the Aegean Bronze Age, the last of the great ages of prehistory recognized by archaeologists.

For the past century it has been customary to divide the prehistoric past into three ages: Stone, Bronze, and Iron. The distinction is based on the principal raw material used to make tools and weapons. Having reviewed the Stone Age in the previous chapters, we are now concerned with the transition to the Age of Bronze, which occurred around 3600 B.C. and took perhaps 500 years.

Simple copper axes, chisels, and pins appear in the latest Neolithic levels of sites in Thessaly, the Peloponnese, and on Crete along with the occasional golden or silver figurine, bead, or bowl. At first these artifacts were very rare and were passed from village to village as curiosities. The earliest examples were made both from native metals panned from rivers and from smelted ore and were no doubt the prized possessions of persons of rank and prestige.

Then as now, the demand for exotic and novel artifacts was the province of the social elite, and the growing use of metal at the end of the Neolithic is a useful indication of the growth of a stratified society

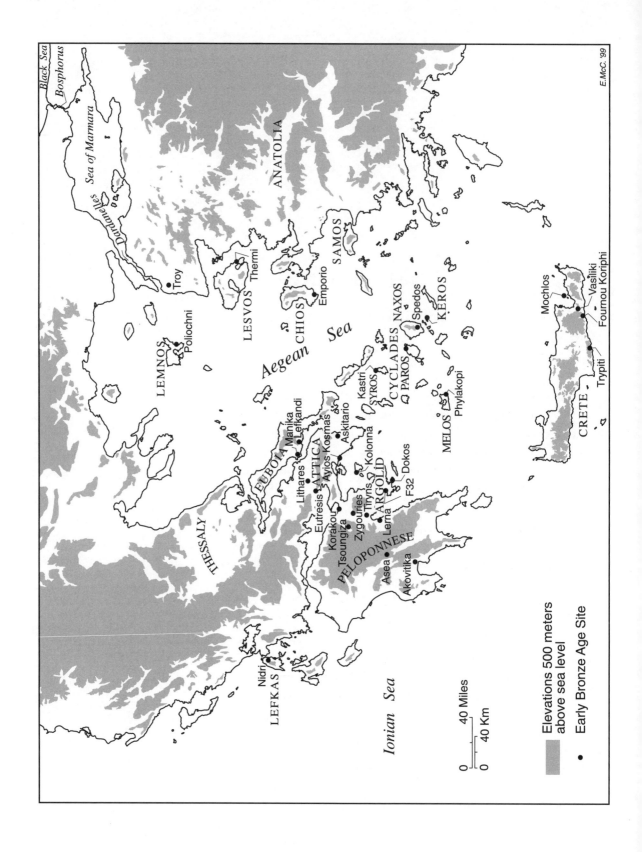

Black Sea

Bosphorus

Sea of Marmara

Dardanelles

ANATOLIA

Troy

Thermi

LESVOS

Poliochni

Emporio

SAMOS

LEMNOS

CHIOS

Aegean Sea

NAXOS

Spedos

KEROS

CYCLADES

Kastri

SYROS

PAROS

Phylakopi

MELOS

THESSALY

EUBOIA

Manika

Lefkandi

Lithares

Avios Kosmas

Eutresis

ATTICA

Askitario

Korakou

Kolonna

Zygouries

Tsoungiza

Tiryns

ARGOLID

Dokos

Lerna

F32

PELOPONNESE

Asea

Akovitika

Nidri

LEFKAS

Ionian Sea

Mochlos

Vasiliki

Fournou Koriphi

Trypiti

CRETE

E.McC. '99

40 Miles

40 Km

0

0

Elevations 500 meters above sea level

• Early Bronze Age Site

with a small elite group at the top. The picture of emerging social complexity is supported by the appearance of large buildings and the construction of fortification walls or at least ditches around many late Neolithic sites. All of these trends were to continue into the Early Bronze Age (hereafter EBA), during which these technological and cultural trends accelerated without a break from the earlier Neolithic period. Figure 4.1 is a map of Early Bronze Age sites.

This view that culture was continuous across the boundary from the Stone Age to the EBA is an important departure from the position of archaeologists during much of the twentieth century. Regional surveys have done much to shift the focus of settlement studies from individual sites to the patterns of settlement in large regions. Whereas earlier excavations concentrated on the identification of the larger sites, regional surveys identify the smaller sites in a hierarchy of settlements that ranged in size from large centers to smaller dependent villages and hamlets. Particularly in the Argolid, survey work showed that the hierarchical structure of settlements began by the beginning of the fourth millennium and continued without interruption into the third millennium. The idea that the Neolithic period was terminated by the abandonment of a large number of sites, perhaps in the face of a migration of new people using the new bronze technology, has itself been abandoned, and current archaeological work focuses on the continuities between the two periods.

The beginning of the Bronze Age is thus entirely arbitrary. The uncertain boundary between the two periods is due in part to the massive rearrangement of many sites in the more developed phase of the EBA. At sites such as Lerna in the Argolid, for instance, the last phases of the Neolithic tell were essentially cut away: the top of the mound was leveled to create more space for large buildings. This same process of cutting and filling at other sites thus did much to obscure the transition. It is nonetheless clear that little by little the use of bronze (an alloy of copper and arsenic, and later, tin) spread through Aegean culture in the form of knives, daggers, axes, and jewelry and became the standard material for tools, weapons, and luxury items by the end

4.1   *Opposite.* The locations of Early Bronze Age sites. This is only a small sample of the better-known and excavated sites. Note their concentration in central Greece, particularly Attica and the Argolid, and that there are more Early Bronze Age sites on the Cyclades and Crete than there are Neolithic sites.

of the fourth millennium B.C. (see Figure 4.2). Chipped stone tools were not entirely supplanted, and the use of Melian obsidian on most mainland sites continued unabated, as did, for a while, the fondness for stone axes. Within a millennium of its first appearance on Aegean sites, however, bronze had become the dominant raw material, and its rise to importance so exactly parallels the growth of complex society in the region that we believe the use of the term "Bronze Age" is fully justified.

A romantic view, and one not supported by archaeological evidence, sees the new EBA culture as the result of invading Indo-Europeans from Central Asia who supplanted an indigenous population of "Old European" Neolithic farmers. A less romantic assessment of the evidence focuses on local changes set in motion long before the Bronze Age. The monumentality of architecture and fortification walls was anticipated at Neolithic sites such as Sesklo and Dimini a thousand years earlier, and most of the other details of material culture were added or subtracted from the basic agricultural economy that supported Neolithic and Bronze Age civilizations. Thus the use of obsidian and pottery continued, bronze weapons were added, and the ever-present Neolithic anthropomorphic figurines disappeared.

The introduction of plow agriculture and seagoing longboats may have been a response to the economic restructuring that affected all of the eastern Mediterranean in the fourth millennium (sometimes called the Secondary Products Revolution, when the production of textiles, cheese, and milk started and animals began to be used for traction and draft). These innovations were perhaps the impetus for other changes

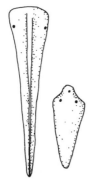

4.2   Two examples of the typical small tin-bronze knives that became common in the Early Bronze Age.

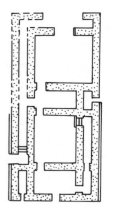

4.3   Plan of the House of the Tiles at Lerna. This so-called corridor house was built on the megaron plan using the essentially Neolithic technology of adobe brick on stone foundations. It was roofed with terra-cotta and split stone tiles and is much larger (nearly 50 meters long) than any of its Neolithic prototypes. It is considered to be a dwelling for members of an important extended family (lineage).

in production and technology throughout Bronze Age material culture. Nothing, however, supports the hypothesis that Greece was invaded or that its population changed in the EBA.

The majority of Early Bronze Age settlements were located in southern Greece, often in conspicuous locations. The Cycladic islands were occupied in earnest, and many of the famous Cycladic marble figurines have been found in large cemeteries on islands such as Syros and Keros. These and changes in almost every aspect of daily life attest to a departure from the ways of the Neolithic past and to the strength and success of the new island culture.

New forms of pottery, usually simple bowls painted red and polished before firing, replaced the figured work of old. The new settlements were large and dominated by well-built houses with complex ground plans. These so-called corridor houses appear to have served as residences for powerful families, or perhaps more accurately lineages composed of several closely related families. These impressive examples of monumental architecture are laid out on the familiar "megaron plan," a rectangular footprint with a front porch bordered by wings and a number of large interior rooms flanked by blind corridors and staircases leading up to (now vanished) second stories. The largest examples exceed 50 meters in length, and, like the House of the Tiles at Lerna, are roofed with fired-clay or cut-stone tiles (see Figure 4.3). The interior walls were sometimes decorated with painted designs or borders in red and black.

More than one lineage dominated the larger settlements, if we are to judge from the presence of two, three, and even more corridor houses at Akovitika near Kalamata in the southern Peloponnese, Lerna in the Argolid, Aigina in the Saronic Gulf, and Troy in northwestern Turkey. The largest sites have strong defensive walls of stone equipped with towers and gates to defend them, and their population may have reached a thousand or more. The largest sites are no more than about ten hectares in area, so they were not really cities (for comparison, the smallest cities in classical times were generally twice as large and populous), but they are too large to be mere villages, and for the lack of a better term we call them towns. We assume that each Bronze Age town was politically independent, something like a small principality or large manorial estate in medieval Europe. Political power was probably wielded by the lineage heads and extended no further than a few hours' walk from the center of town (see Figure 4.4).

The emergence of proto-urban life in Early Bronze Age towns

was accompanied by profound economic changes. The plow pulled by oxen was introduced to work the fields, and the primeval forest was cut down in many areas to open up new and larger fields suitable for plow agriculture. As the plow made possible a rain-dependent agriculture and vastly increased the capacity of the land to support a growing population, people moved across the landscape to form networks of interdependent communities of different sizes. The expansion of settlement across the landscape documented by many archaeological surveys, and the continued practice of forest clearance, led to soil erosion, in some regions on a catastrophic scale. As the EBA progressed in the third millennium the initial expansion of settlement was halted, and eventually some settlements on the higher slopes and upland valleys had to be abandoned; their residents moved to the valley bottoms where eroded sediments from the higher elevations had accumulated, making farming possible there.

The process can be followed in detail in the Argolid, where surveys of the southern Argolid, and of the Berbati and Nemea Valleys in the north, have brought to light a pattern of settlement that began in the later Neolithic, expanded in the Middle and Late Neolithic periods, and accelerated in the EBA. In the Berbati Valley and southern Argolid, although not in Nemea, the Final Neolithic was a period of stable Late Stone Age life. Farming and herding activity, as revealed by the

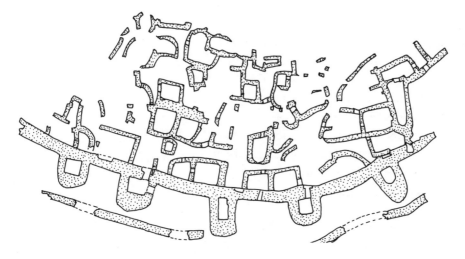

4.4 Plan of a small fortified Early Cycladic town on the island of Syros. The organization of the fortification wall with its tower and outer wall controlling access to the central gate contrasts markedly with the higgledy-piggledy plan of the houses inside.

presence of axes, sickle elements, spindle whorls, and querns, took place high in the hills and deep in the interior valleys, sometimes on slopes that are today stripped of soil.

The following phases of the EBA (known as Early Helladic, or EH I and II in archaeological jargon) cannot be traced successively on any one excavated site, but there was clearly a population shift from the hills to the fertile valley bottoms. The timing of this movement was different in the two parts of the Argolid, but in both areas the human population movement coincided with the geological evidence that soil began eroding from the slopes in the Final Neolithic—EH I period and accelerated in the early third millennium. That it was over by the time the fully developed EH II sites were founded is amply demonstrated by the discovery of EH II sites sitting on top of the sediments that had washed into the valley bottoms. After this rather major rearrangement of the landscape, which was likely brought about primarily by farming practices and forest clearing and secondarily by climate change, EH sites remained closely connected with the valley bottoms. The settlements in the higher elevations and more remote interior valleys were abandoned. This state of affairs persisted until the end of the period, around 2000 B.C.

LIFE IN THE EARLY BRONZE AGE

Spiritually and artistically, the Early Bronze Age was significant. Rather inexplicably, the human figurines so popular in the Neolithic period disappeared from the mainland. Only a handful of animal figurines of clay enliven the EBA repertoire, and they usually depict common domestic animals like sheep or cows. Although these may have been mere toys, on the analogy with later classical Greek religion it is likely that these are votive offerings to the gods. Their use may reflect the growing importance of herding in the economy. Even today, small silver plaques depicting domestic animals can be found on icons in country churches.

Human figures continued to be made in the Cycladic islands, but these enigmatic and startlingly modern figurines are very different from Neolithic figurines. They were carved from island marble, which has a crystalline white color and looks like sparkling sugar on its unpolished surface. They were carved and polished using locally available emery, a diamond-hard mineral. The Cycladic idols, as they are called, are thought to have had some kind of cultic use, particularly because of their standardized form and frequency of occurrence in EBA tombs (see Figure 4.5). Although many, but not all, seem to be of nude females with bent knees, downward-pointing toes, and arms crossed over the stomach, the many variations on this theme point away from a single meaning for all of them. The sculptures range in size from miniature to near life-size and are sometimes single figures, sometimes two or more figures joined together head to foot. Rarely they are equipped with belts and daggers, or are seated on chairs with musical instruments. These Cycladic idols do not tell us much about EBA religious practice. No cult buildings or temples have been clearly identified; religion appears to have been practiced at the level of the household and is particularly conspicuous in connection with burials. On the mainland, burial was by interment, but sometimes several people were buried together and covered with a mound of earth.

Considering the wide range of male and female deities worshiped in neighboring Mesopotamia and Egypt at this time, we can suppose that the Aegean peoples worshiped a large pantheon of gods. Some of the gods familiar from classical Greece appear already in the Linear B tablets from Late Bronze Age times (ca. 1450 B.C.), and some conti-

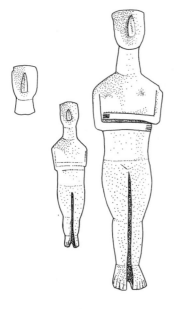

4.5 Early Cycladic anthropomorphic figurines and larger statues with folded arms were carved out of local marble. Cycladic idols have been collected by European connoisseurs for 200 years, but few of the known examples have come from controlled archaeological excavations. As a consequence, little is known about their meaning or function.

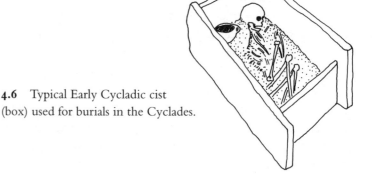

4.6 Typical Early Cycladic cist (box) used for burials in the Cyclades.

nuity of cult may yet be demonstrated. But for now a respectful silence must prevail on the subject.

In the Cycladic islands EBA culture has distinctive regional characteristics; it is known as Early Cycladic (EC) to distinguish it from the Helladic culture of the mainland. Early Cycladic burials took place in clearly demarcated cemeteries; the deceased were laid in stone-lined boxes called cists (see Figure 4.6).

Incised drawings on Early Cycladic pottery and a few rare models in lead depict longboats that resemble dugouts or large canoes. They were likely made of wooden planks, and the illustrations show them being propelled by teams of rowers. These longboats helped connect the settlements on the Cycladic islands with the coastal mainland sites and establish the distinctive marine orientation of all later Greek cultures. They were also pivotal in the expansion of trade in metals (gold, silver, copper, and lead), which were mined from the rich deposits at Lavrion, near Athens, and on the islands of Serifos and Siphnos. Other items of trade included sharp volcanic obsidian from Melos for cutting tools, gritty lava from the other islands used in querns to grind flour, marble for bowls and figurines, and other commodities both durable and perishable that can only be guessed at, such as textiles, salt, and wood.

The trade in both tangible materials and perishable substances fueled an international network of traders and peddlers who moved goods and ideas around the shores of the Aegean Sea. A profusion of clay sealings (pieces of clay used to close containers) from sites of this period bear impressions from seals of stone or other material. These sealings, which bear the marks of cords and basketry, were broken from boxes, baskets, or necks of pots, proving that goods were stored in Early Helladic sites on the mainland. Seals probably served as marks of ownership, but it is not known whether the seal designs bore some form of writing or reflected an accounting system. Seals could have been combined with potters' marks and other scratched signs to form a script similar to later Linear A and B. There is no clear connection, however, between the EBA and Late Bronze Age (LBA) writing systems, and we are forced to conclude that the EBA communities, so civilized in other ways, were essentially illiterate.

The distinctive EBA culture flourished around the Aegean Sea. Distinctive artifacts like the so-called sauceboats in painted clay or beaten gold and the unmistakable white marble Cycladic idols have prompted some archaeologists to describe Aegean EBA culture as having an "international spirit" (see Figure 4.7). The foundations of the later Mycenaean-Minoan civilization were laid down in this period, as the centers of power were established in the southeastern portion of the mainland, on the islands, and on Crete. Typical features were its fortified citadels, monumental, even palatial, dwellings for a powerful social elite, and an intense interest in novel bronze weapons and their display.

Perhaps the most dynamic contribution of the EBA culture to later cultures was plow agriculture. Rapid population growth followed (or perhaps caused) the opening of fields in the previously unused forest. The EBA culture endured in some areas for a millennium; its phases are distinguished by the rebuilding of architecture at most sites and by minor changes in pottery and other artifacts (see Figures 4.8–9). It came to an end in a blaze of site destructions that began about 2250 B.C. and continued off and on for a century or more.

Many sites were abandoned, and some areas, especially in the Cyclades, may even have been depopulated. The disruption at the end of the EBA occurred around the Aegean, in Asia Minor as well as in Greece. At Troy, the violent destruction of the EBA settlement of Troy II (the second settlement in the sequence of nine superimposed settlements at Troy) was one of the reasons that Heinrich Schliemann

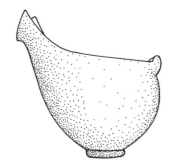

4.7   The terra-cotta "sauceboat" is a common artifact on the mainland in the Early Helladic period, but its function is unknown. It is very common in the second phase of the Early Helladic (ca. 2700–2300 B.C.), and fragments of these vessels are found on the surface of almost every site in this period. Whatever it was used for it must have been important: at least two versions in gold have turned up, and there were possibly others in silver and bronze.

4.8   Terra-cotta "frying pans" are typical finds of the Early Cycladic culture in the islands. Of unknown use, they are often decorated with spirals, scratched images of oared longboats, and sometimes, curiously, little legs and female genitalia as in this example.

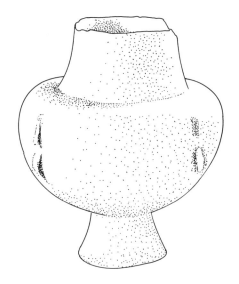

4.9 Early Cycladic marble ateliers produced a wide range of marble vessels. This one has lug handles useful for tying the ends of a leather or cloth cover over the vessel.

mistook this level for Homeric Troy. The destruction level belongs instead to a catastrophe a thousand years before the Trojan War.

Material culture changed dramatically in the centuries after the Early Bronze Age collapsed, particularly on the mainland. Evidence of new house forms, grave types, and styles of decorated pottery have encouraged the interpretation that population movements accompanied the wave of destructions. There is good reason to see the influence of Asia Minor in the black-and-red-faced pottery tankards that replaced the older sauceboats and other EBA pottery types. Many of the pottery forms prevalent in the phases following the EBA had long been known in western Anatolia. But the parallels are rarely exact. Some aspects of the pottery found on the Greek mainland are distinctive and may have been produced locally. Thus some movements were probably more local.

Whatever the cause, the first Bronze Age civilization vanished in flames and obscurity and was followed by a period of retrenchment. On the mainland and in the Cyclades a few of the larger villages continued to pursue a reduced version of civilized agricultural life for half a millennium during the so-called Middle Helladic period (called Middle Cycladic on the islands and Middle Minoan on Crete). Huddled behind their walls, these villages differed little from their Neolithic forebears. Advancement and change seem to have been limited to experiments in pottery production with the newly introduced potter's wheel and the manufacture of complex forms in stone.

CRETE AND THE MINOAN CIVILIZATION

On the big island of Crete, however, things were different. Shortly after the end of the Early Bronze Age in the Aegean, a novel cultural trend got under way on Crete. The pioneer archaeologist Sir Arthur Evans called the Cretan EBA culture by its own regional name, Early Minoan, to distinguish it from the later Middle and Late Minoan periods when the great palaces dominated the island (see Figure 4.1).

The distinctive feature of the Early Minoan (EM) culture is that it may have escaped the destructive ravages that overwhelmed the majority of Aegean sites between 2250 and 2000 B.C. Although some EM sites were evidently abandoned, and others may have been damaged by fire (such as Vasiliki on the Ierapetra Isthmus) or completely destroyed, we do not know what fate they suffered at the end of the period. Part of the problem is that many Early Minoan sites lie beneath the Middle and Late Minoan palaces (ca. 2000–1380 B.C.). The sprawling palace complexes at Knossos, Mallia, and Phaistos are known to have earlier phases, but these cannot be investigated systematically without removing the later structures, which are of great archaeological, architectural, and touristic importance. Other sites, such as the palatial remains beneath the city of Chania in western Crete and the site of Archanes, south of Knossos, are obscured by numerous modern buildings.

Nevertheless, we believe that there was a more or less continuous development of culture across the divide between the last phase of the Early Minoan period and the beginning of the Middle Minoan, when the distinctive and very sophisticated Minoan culture of the so-called Palace Period took shape. It seems that the size of the island, and perhaps its distance from the mainlands of Greece and Anatolia were sufficient to buffer the Minoan culture during the turbulent centuries that followed the EH II–EC II cultural peak, allowing the island culture to flourish in those trying times.

Early Minoan sites of importance are the small villages of Fournou Koriphi, Mochlos, Debla, and the newly discovered Ayios Konstantinos. More complex architectural remains of a larger village are located at Vasiliki, and a major cemetery is found on the island of Mochlos. The typical EM settlements, if it is possible to generalize with a limited sample, were small villages with a jumble of roughly rectangular dwellings with stone foundations and mud-brick superstructures. The availability of materials and setting affected building construction. At Mochlos, houses were built from metamorphic rocks that split into convenient slabs, permitting high-quality work. At Fournou Koriphi, on the southern end of the Ierapetra Isthmus, the foundations of local field stones of irregular size are formed into only very roughly rectilinear foundations. Vasiliki appears to have had several buildings of imposing size and quality around one or more paved courtyards. These buildings seem to have been rebuilt periodically, and were occupied during several different phases. As on the mainland, there seems to have been a simple hierarchy of settlements, with some larger, wealthier sites at the top of the system. The finds from the Mochlos cemetery reinforce the picture of unequally distributed wealth at this time.

Burial practices on Crete were extremely varied. The rectangular chamber tombs of Mochlos investigated by the American archaeologist Richard Seager early in the twentieth century resemble the houses on the same small island. The tombs had multiple burials and were richly appointed with pottery, stone vessels, and some jewelry of colored stones and gold (see Figure 4.10). The tombs appear to have served the members of a single family or lineage.

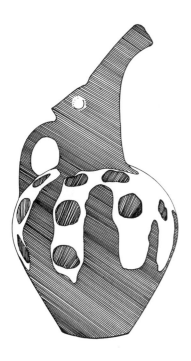

4.10   Vasiliki ware (named after the site on the Ierapetra Isthmus where it was first found) is the typical pottery production of the Early Minoan period. The distinctive mottled decoration is thought to imitate the appearance of contemporary stone or metallic vessels. The perky bird-beak spout recalls Cycladic forms and can be traced to the Anatolian highlands directly across the Aegean.

In sharp contrast, in much of the southern part of Crete, for instance the Mesara Plain around Phaistos, round, free-standing vaulted structures called *tholos* tombs appear to have been community sepulchers with sometimes dozens of people buried in them (*tholos* is the Greek word for a round building). Large quantities of grave goods in the *tholoi* (plural of *tholos*) include bronze weapons, ivory seals, and jewelry made from exotic materials. All of the grave fields were used continuously from the Early to the Middle Minoan period, apparently overlapping with the earliest palaces of the later period.

A full picture of the spiritual and artistic world of Early Minoan Crete can be pieced together only with great difficulty. The tombs tell us that the treatment of the dead and reverence for ancestors was of great importance in the EM cult. Clay figurines of animals and Cycladic marble figurines may be linked with island systems of belief, and may even establish the presence of Cycladic islanders in Crete. The figurine of a rather dumpy female carrying a pitcher, which was found in the village remains of Fournou Koriphi, has been classified as a devotional figurine of some kind, chiefly on the comparison with such figurines in later Minoan society and elsewhere around the Mediterranean. A ceramic figure in the form of a bull, which was an object of veneration in cultures from Neolithic Çatal Höyük in Turkey to Bronze Age Egypt, suggests that the animal interested the Early Minoans as well.

Perhaps the most significant artistic achievements of the Early Minoans are the everyday artifacts that have been recovered from tombs. The specialized and highly skilled craft of making bronze weapons was practiced on the island, as was the manufacture of vessels from rare and exotic types of stone (a form of craft specialization that originated in Egypt, to judge from some of the shapes that inspired the Minoan pieces). Finds of ivory seals and gemstones suggest that the EM culture participated in Aegean-wide, if not larger, spheres of craft specialization and economic activity. This conclusion is supported by the abundance of imported Melian obsidian found at most sites.

The apparent integration of the EM economy with the Cycladic and mainland cultures is perhaps significant. The Minoans may have been in a favored geographic position to survive the disruptions at the end of the EBA and to turn their attention to trade and cultural interaction with their other near neighbors in Egypt and the Levant.

The Age of Palaces

The justly famous Minoan palaces have been the objects of archaeological enthusiasm, touristic excitement, and amateur zeal ever since their discovery by Sir Arthur Evans a century ago (see Figure 4.11). Efforts to explain their function and meaning are ongoing, but one thing is clear: they owe little or nothing to the architectural heritage of the Bronze Age Aegean and are a truly original native creation. Consisting of large, sprawling complexes of rooms surrounding a big central courtyard, the palaces once had elevations of five or even six stories and were designed for comfortable living. The residential character of the palaces is the defining feature of Minoan monumental architecture. The large palaces eschew any obvious arrangements for defense, a fact that has led researchers to conclude that life in the Palace Period was peaceful and secure. For a typical palace plan, see Figure 4.12.

The date of the earliest palace foundations is unknown. The main palaces at Mallia, Knossos, and Phaistos were evidently laid out early in the Middle Minoan period, around 2000 B.C. Over the next 600 years, the palaces were constructed, partially destroyed, and reconstructed again before they were destroyed for good around 1450 B.C.

4.11 The locations of the principal Minoan sites on Crete.

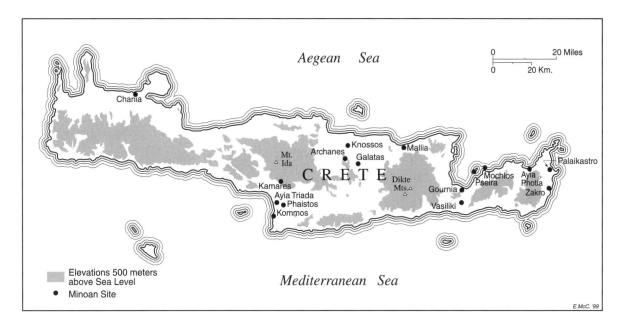

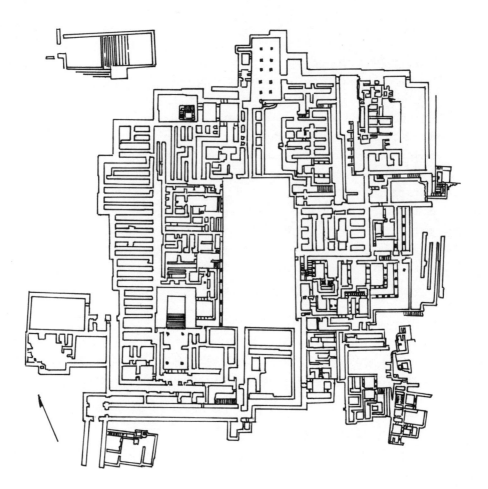

4.12   Plan of the Palace of Minos at Knossos. All the known Minoan palaces share many of the features seen here at Knossos, such as the western courtyard, the long parallel magazines, the central courtyard, the rambling domestic apartments on the east, and the lack of a formal entrance or encircling fortifications. Knossos is the largest of the palaces. The other palaces on Crete have their own idiosyncrasies but resemble Knossos in the main, which suggests that later builders imitated the oldest and greatest palace but also maintained an independence of spirit that filters into the details of local design. The plan of the palace is very sophisticated, calling to mind the intricacy of a modern computer chip. Note its resemblance also to a self-contained village layout; indeed the building is nothing more than a village under one roof. Several phases of building over a period of several hundred years are visible at the site; we show here the last phase of the building, ca. 1400 B.C., shortly before its final destruction.

It is difficult to untangle the architectural history of the palaces where later constructions cover the earlier foundations. The collapse of the palaces and the partial survival of Minoan culture after 1450 B.C. is equally murky. Although a limited form of Minoan culture may have continued as late as 1200 B.C. at some sites (most notably Knossos), and even later at the mountain site of Karphi, the great period of cultural fluorescence occurred before 1450 B.C., and the aftermath was but a pale reflection of earlier glory.

By the classical period, knowledge of Minoan culture was reduced to a patchwork of myths and legends surrounding Minos, the once-upon-a-time king of Knossos, and until the startling revelations of Arthur Evans's excavations in 1900, Minoan culture was no more than legend.

Resembling large villages grouped together to form a single architectural complex, the Minoan palaces have fueled speculation about their functions and about the nature and character of the Minoan palace society. The designation "palace" is itself controversial. Archaeologists use "palace" in an entirely conventional manner as a traditional label for a ruler's residence, but there is little reason to believe the palaces housed a monarch in the modern sense of the term as an individual head of state. Although some writers have argued that the palaces were temples or mortuary complexes, such explanations carry little weight with archaeologists. The palaces are best explained as residences (in part) for a fairly large group of people. The residents were probably the members of an extended elite lineage, whose precise composition is of course unknown and which may have mixed the functions of priests and princes. This conclusion is based on the analogous use of large palaces in the Near East and Egypt as residences for ruling families and their dependents and relatives. It will be useful to take a look at the palaces in more detail before turning to an analysis of Minoan culture as a whole.

The clearest picture of a Minoan palace can be seen at Knossos, where Sir Arthur Evans reconstructed substantial portions of the structure. The outer walls of the palace were built in part of cut stone blocks in the lower courses; the upper walls were made of plaster-covered rubble, which also served for interior divisions. The airy, open interior rooms were decorated with colorful wall paintings depicting humans, monkeys, plants, and marine motifs in hues of red, blue, yellow, and white (see Figures 4.13 and 4.14). The spacious rooms have numerous windows and doors and few clever or fussy additions. They are mostly square or rectangular.

Sir Arthur Evans took pride in the superb drainage system and up-to-date hydraulic system of the Palace of Minos, which provided ample drinking and bathing water and even allowed a flush toilet or two. Lighting was ensured by a system of windows, light wells (openings to the sky that pass through the fabric of the building), and strategically placed stone oil lamps. All the palaces provided ample room for the storage of goods and supplies and comfortable living quarters for their residents. Apart from the central courtyards, a palace had no focal point or center, and the visitor familiar with modern royal residences will note the absence of large audience halls, throne rooms (except one late addition at Knossos, which is probably Mycenaean), or other features required by present-day monarchs. The palaces more closely resemble the sprawling compounds of decentralized function that are characteristic of Near Eastern complexes from the Bronze Age to the great Ottoman palace of Topkapi Sarayi in Istanbul. The upper floors of most of the palaces have been destroyed, leaving only the foundations. An idea of the appearance of the buildings can be

4.13   An octopus from a painted pot in the Marine style. Such motifs found their way in the New Palace Period onto pots, wall paintings (frescoes), gems, seals, and other artwork.

4.14   Dolphins from a fresco in the Palace of Minos at Knossos mirror the motifs found in Marine-style pottery.

gained from wall paintings and other artworks (see Figure 4.15). Audience halls or royal chambers may have occupied the upper floors, but this kind of speculation does not take us very far.

Let us now look at the progressive development of the palaces of Crete that stand at the heart of Minoan civilization. All of the palaces were built and rebuilt on a few carefully selected sites: Knossos, Mallia, Zakro, Phaistos, Ayia Triada, Gournia, Palaikastro, and Chania. Although the plans of the palaces are very similar, some are considerably larger than others, and Knossos is the largest and most complex of them all. The palaces did not stand alone but were situated in the midst of a variety of architectural dependencies. The complex at Knossos appears to have consisted of private residences (variously referred to as mansions or villas), cult centers, and mortuary complexes. The numerous outbuildings around the palace at Mallia include underground pillared rooms. These and other unusual features defy ready explanation. At no site has the entire range of dependent structures been investigated completely by excavation.

None of the palace complexes can be reasonably described as "towns" or "cities" except the small palace complex at Gournia. It stands at the center of a compact, practical, and rather cozy little village devoted to agriculture and small-time village crafts such as carpentry and blacksmithing. Others, particularly Knossos and Mallia, have a bewildering array of buildings, tombs, roads, and other structures that defy easy classification or interpretation. No two complexes seem to have any specific similarities, aside from the palaces themselves, but the larger palaces may have supported craftsmen, much like the village of Gournia, to produce fancy metalwork, frescoes, pottery, stone vessels, and other crafts (see Figures 4.16–4.20).

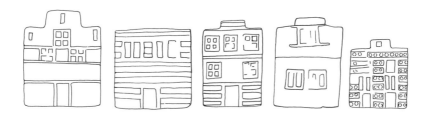

4.15 These small plaques of faience (a type of glass made from crushed quartz paste with a blue-green alkaline glaze) from Knossos were originally furniture inlays, but they permit us to visualize the appearance of the facades of Minoan buildings.

4.16 This gold jewel from Mallia is an example of the high quality of goldsmithing at the Minoan palaces at a very early period (ca. 1800–1600 B.C.).

4.17 The famous Toreador fresco from Knossos illustrating Minoan bull leapers. The content of this painting has been debated for decades. Two of the figures are female, and the third, vaulting over the back of the bull, is male. They are all dressed alike. The bull is shown galloping to the left, but the two figures at either end are in stationary positions. Does the action depict a sport, a bull sacrifice, human sacrifice, or a scene from myth or poetic literature? It is simply not possible to know for sure.

4.18 A Marine-style pottery vessel. This style of pottery was in vogue between 1500 and 1450 B.C. and is quintessentially Minoan.

Although the origins of the palaces are obscure, careful attention to the different levels and phases of building (such as successive floors, walls upon walls, blocked-up doors, and rubble-filled hallways) makes it possible to discern two great periods of palace construction. During the Old Palace Period the palaces were first laid out with a central courtyard and mazelike room pattern that persisted to the end of Minoan civilization itself.

The exact details of the first palaces will always be hard to make out because the later palaces were built directly over them. At Phaistos in the south and at Knossos, limited test excavations have provided the best picture of an older palace. Great attention was given to its western facade, no doubt to create the best and grandest approach to the palace across a paved, west-facing courtyard. The interior arrangements included long subterranean storage magazines (see Figure 4.21), the central court, and apartments. The old palaces were decorated with

4.19 A finely shaped, high-quality stone vessel from the small palace at Zakro. Stone vases of breccia, porphyry, marble, alabaster, and rock crystal are common at the palaces.

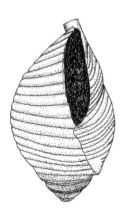

4.20 A stone vessel in the shape of a marine shell carved from obsidian, a quartz-hard volcanic rock, one of at least four found on Crete. This is technically one of the finest-quality vessels from the Minoan world. Similar obsidian vases are known from the Near East, and Egypt's ancient tradition of producing fine stone vessels allows us to place the Minoan taste for these fascinating objects within the context of eastern Mediterranean luxury goods. Items such as this were exported, displayed in the palaces, or used in religious ceremonies.

wall paintings (frescoes), and the material culture was similar to that of the next phase.

The old palaces were destroyed in an island-wide catastrophe about 1700 B.C. The fact that they were all immediately rebuilt indicates that the catastrophe was natural, most probably a severe earthquake. The new palaces appear to have been built according to the same plan as the old and more or less directly over their predecessors (except at Phaistos, where the palace was rebuilt a few meters to the east, leaving part of the old palace exposed for excavation).

The palaces of the New Palace Period constitute the bulk of the preserved remains visible today. The visible remains and most of the textbook descriptions of the Minoan palaces (including this one to some extent) refer to only the last phase of the Minoan palaces. The frescoes, pottery, figurines, and general appearance of the existing architecture at the best-known site of Knossos belong entirely to the last generation of occupation of the palace, a time when most of the other palaces were already out of use. Whether this picture of Minoan culture and its inhabitants is similar to that of the earlier palaces and peoples remains a matter of some debate.

The new palaces were rebuilt on a more substantial and luxurious plan than the old ones, and the generous use of square-cut stone in the foundations is particularly noticeable, especially for the western facades. A lovely translucent, pearly alabaster was used extensively to line the inner walls and to embellish the living chambers and baths. And frescoes depicted lively scenes from court life, the famous bull-leaping motif (Fig. 4.17), scenes probably of religious content, and a wide variety of naturalistic themes illustrating flowered gardens, monkeys in open landscapes, dolphins, octopus, fish, and other marine life.

The 200 years or so of the New Palace Period produced a succession of distinctive pottery styles with general decorative themes, such as the Floral style and the Marine style. The best of the pottery is of outstanding artistic quality, as are many of the figurines of ivory, gold, and faience (colored glass), carved gems, and sculpted stone vessels (Figs. 4.18–4.20). We shall turn below to a discussion of the religious,

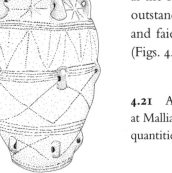

4.21 A large pithos, or storage jar, from the magazines at Mallia. Such vessels, some over six feet tall, held large quantities of olive oil, grain, and other foodstuffs.

political, and economic aspects of Minoan life, but if we knew nothing more about them than what we can see in their architecture and material culture, we would admire the Minoans for the accomplishments of the New Palace Period.

Despite their obvious cultural success and the 600-year duration of the Palatial civilization, Minoan culture was not to survive. A second catastrophe around 1450 B.C. swept across the island, obliterated the palaces, and all but annihilated the entire culture. Almost all of the palaces were destroyed by fire, although one or two (Knossos and perhaps Phaistos and Chania) survived for another 80 or 90 years, but in very altered circumstances. Many scholars attribute the destruction of the Minoan palaces to an invasion from the mainland, presumably by the Mycenaean Greeks. The chief evidence for this is the Linear B tablets that came into use at Knossos and significant remodeling of the Palace of Minos at Knossos, where a throne room was added. A new style of painted pottery (the Palace style) was introduced along with new mortuary customs that emphasized interment with military gear of the mainland style.

The Mycenaeans made the surviving palace of Knossos their base for exploiting the conquered island. Even so, the Knossos palace was destroyed for a second time in a violent conflagration. After this last disaster, Minoan civilization was all but over. Like the Maya in Central America, the Minoans abandoned the palatial centers and scattered across the island in small agricultural villages, where, again like the present-day Maya, their descendents are still to be found. Late Minoan and Sub-Minoan villages in the mountains of central Crete, like Karphi south of Mallia, had no palaces, but they may have continued to worship Minoan deities. Terra-cotta figurines of females with upraised arms and crowned with poppies were deposited in small, rustic shrines. By the dawn of recorded Greek history in the eighth century B.C., however, all that was left of the great Minoan civilization was to be found only in legend, myth, and buried ruins.

DISTINCTIVE FEATURES OF MINOAN CULTURE

The world of the Minoans was centered on the palaces but included many other features as well. An intricate and highly organized network of roads on the island linked villages, isolated houses called "villas," cult centers in caves and mountain peaks, and even a few rather curious fortified houses. Examples of nearly all of these features can been seen or visited by the serious traveler with a car and a sense of adventure.

The village of Gournia on the Ierapetra Isthmus in eastern Crete is perhaps the best place to see what Minoan life was like outside the great palaces. Gournia resembled a medieval town clustered around its own little palace for comfort or protection. Its winding streets have no obvious plan; the village seems to have been there first and the palace added only later. Without the palace, it could be a village of almost any period. It was excavated by the remarkable American archaeologist Harriet Boyd Hawes in 1906–1908. There she found tools and equipment belonging to evidently prosperous farmers living in solidly built stone houses.

This village provides a picture of the Minoan economy, which was chiefly agricultural, based on the cultivation of wheat, barley, sheep, goats, pigs, and cattle. The olive was known, if not as widely used as in later times, and grapes provided wine. The donkey was domesticated in this period to provide transportation of goods and traction for carts and plows. There is also evidence of substantial craft specialization based on imported raw materials such as bronze, ivory, rock crystal, and colored stone. Trade was evidently an important part of the Minoan economy both inside the palaces and out. The craft items produced at Gournia and in the palace workshops were in part made from imported raw materials such as Syrian ivory, Egyptian gold, and Cypriot copper. Objects of undoubted Minoan manufacture were good enough to grace the halls of the Egyptian pharaohs, as can be determined from Minoan finds in Egypt and Egyptian wall paintings.

The importation of raw materials by ship has been well documented in the past two or three decades by the spectacular discovery of Bronze Age shipwrecks with their cargoes off the southern coast of Turkey. Although the shipwrecks of Cape Gelidonya and Uluburun belong to a later period than the last Minoan palaces, similar cargoes of copper, ebony wood, ivory, and glass paste must have made their rounds in the heyday of the palaces. It is clear that the palaces bristled with craft workshops, and the small palace at Kato Zakro, which escaped looting after its fifteenth-century B.C. destruction, had ample supplies in its storerooms of unworked copper and elephant ivory necessary to keep the craftsmen going.

The entire island economy appears to have been organized around the palaces. Some of the storage magazines and remains of workshops still contain stockpiles of raw materials, such as the beautiful green breccia (a stone used for vessels) visible in a room in the northeast wing at Knossos. Clay tablets with writing in an undeciphered hieroglyphic script provide evidence of a record-keeping system. So-called Linear A, one of two scripts used on Crete, was undoubtedly used to record the Minoan language and is clearly connected with economic record keeping. Pictograms on the tablets depict easily recognized commodities such as pots, wheat, and sheep, and these are paired with slashes and dots indicating numerals. Thus the accounting function of the tablets can be determined with certainty, although the language they are written in is unknown. A great many people, not least of whom was Sir Arthur Evans himself, have endeavored to decipher Linear A, so far without success. The second script, Linear B, was used in the last phase of the Knossos palace to write a form of Greek and is described later.

If Linear A were ever deciphered it might be possible to say something concrete about Minoan government, social organization, and religious belief. As it is, we are forced to hazard conjectures about these subjects that can be supported with archaeological artifacts or artistic representations.

More has probably been written about Minoan religion than almost any other aspect of Minoan culture. There is a long tradition of attempting to use the familiar gods and goddesses of much later classical Greek myth and cult to interpret Minoan religious art and artifacts, but we have always found this to be a questionable practice at best.

The Minoans lived a thousand years before the classical age, and it is not certain that they were ethnically or linguistically similar to the later inhabitants of the Greek mainland. During the considerable interval that separated the high Minoan culture from the earliest recorded expressions of Greek religion, much was changed or lost in transmission, and there is no evidence of any close correspondence between the two. (See the Bibliographic Essay for some suggested reading on this difficult subject.) Briefly, however, Minoan cult practice was carried out in high mountain-peak sanctuaries, within deep caverns, at tombs, and to some extent within the palaces themselves. On the high mountain peaks, shrines with altars were used to make offerings and sacrifices to one or more deities. Small figurines in clay, metal, or ivory were often dedicated at these shrines; they depict men and women in a stylized posture, perhaps the worshipers themselves, although sometimes priests and priestesses may be represented (see Figure 4.22). Other dedications include little arms and other body parts, much like votives in modern Christian churches. Gold double axes and other miniatures turn up at the most important shrines (see Figure 4.23).

In all the Minoan cult places there is a persistent emphasis on animals, with the bull and wild goat being favorites (see Figure 4.24).

4.22   A cast bronze figurine of a male wearing a kilt and holding his hand in an attitude thought to represent prayer or worship. Such figurines have been found in votive deposits at mountain-peak sanctuaries.

4.23   A small golden double axe from a votive deposit in a shrine. The double axe was an important symbol of Minoan palatial culture, but the finer points of its meaning elude us.

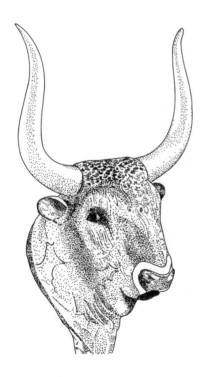

4.24   A bull's head rhyton, or ritual vessel, from Knossos. This fine, dark green serpentine vessel has a small opening at the neck and an exit hole in the mouth, presumably to permit libations to be poured. It seems certain that this was an important ceremonial vessel. The exact meaning of the bull symbolism is unknown, but it may have been used as part of a religious cult.

Stylized bulls' horns are often depicted, and large "Horns of Conse-cration" were mounted on the eaves of the palaces and other large buildings. The most famous use of bulls in Minoan art is found in the curious bull-leaping frescoes from Knossos. These almost certainly have religious significance.

Other intriguing finds are the little faience figurines of women in elaborate dresses with outstretched arms found at Knossos from the Old Palace Period (see Figure 4.25). These figures are of standing females with bare breasts, large hats, elaborate flounced skirts with colored aprons, and handfuls of snakes. The Knossos examples were found with a clutch of stones and shells from what was presumed to be

4.25 This magnificent but partly reconstructed small figurine of faience was found in the Temple Repository at Knossos by Sir Arthur Evans. With her courtly costume of flounced skirt and open bodice, snakes in outstretched hands, and wearing a floppy beret with some kind of feline ornament, she may represent a priestess or a worshiper from a palace shrine.

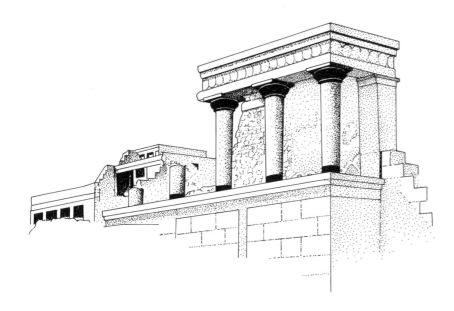

4.26 View of the remaining ruins of the north entrance to the Palace of Minos at Knossos.

a kind of shrine deposit (left over after a shrine was ritually "cleaned"). There is no consensus on the meaning of these evocative and intriguing objects; here, as above, if we appear to be avoiding any interpretation, it is because we want to avoid the excessive unfounded speculation that invests this subject.

The mountain-peak and cavern shrines are on all parts of the island and show a uniformity of belief and practice, proving that there was one body of religious belief (rather than many). The palaces and settlements may have had small shrines, but Minoan settlements lack the grand temples that are so conspicuous in the neighboring Mesopotamian and Egyptian cultures (see Figure 4.26).

If religion is a tough nut to crack, Minoan political organization is no more revealing. Sir Arthur Evans wanted to place a king on the throne at Knossos, but the stone seat he found in the western wing, if it is even a throne in the modern meaning of the term, was in any case

4.27 The Throne Room at Knossos as reconstructed by Sir Arthur Evans. Although the throne itself is called the "oldest throne in Europe" and the "Throne of Minos," the throne room was a later addition to the palace during the last phase of occupation after 1450 B.C. The wall decoration recalls that found in the throne room at Pylos in the Peloponnese, a comparison reinforced by the similarity of the Linear B tablets at the two palaces. It is important evidence for a Mycenaean presence on Crete at the end of the fifteenth century B.C.

a later Mycenaean addition, and the legendary King Minos was, well, a legend (see Figure 4.27). Evans called Knossos the Palace of Minos, and the appellation has stuck, but most scholars today are not convinced that a king or queen headed the Minoan hierarchy. What evidence is there for royalty, after all, once we subtract the palace and testimony of the Homeric poems? Where are the depictions of royal persons? Where are the emblems of a royal house? Is the bull a sign of royalty? Is the double axe a sign of the ruler? Bluntly stated, we do not have any evidence of the form of governance that was practiced, and do not know if the various palaces were separate political entities or were controlled from one palace, such as Knossos. Consensus, however, favors some form of principality, though not necessarily a kingdom with royalty in the modern sense.

All the neighboring polities, after all, from Egypt to the Hittites, were governed by a monarch of some sort. The experts can tell us more, and of course if one day a Linear A archive is found and deciphered, it will explain the workings of the Minoan state(s). But certainty about these things is not necessary to appreciate the complexity and originality of Minoan culture.

Another, less glorious, side of Minoan civilization must be confronted as well. Archaeological discoveries in the 1980s and 1990s at Knossos and Archanes in central Crete have brought to light evidence of human sacrifice and infant cannibalism. At Archanes a shrine destroyed by an earthquake preserves the remains of a sacrificial victim (a young man). Children's bones were found at Knossos with animal bones, both showing signs of butchery and cooking. These finds bring to mind the ancient Greek myths and legends concerning Minos that contain graphic accounts of violence and human sacrifice, particularly the account of Minos's war against Athens and his annual tribute of human sacrifices to sate the appetite of the monstrous Minotaur imprisoned in the Labyrinth of Knossos. Even if we doubt the myths, many of the frescoes and ivories of the acrobatic bull may depict some form of human sacrifice.

There is otherwise a striking absence of military hardware in Minoan art. Weapons are only rarely found at the palaces (at least outside Knossos), and there is no reason to think that the Minoans were concerned about external foes or an organized invasion of their island. In this they were gravely mistaken, and the destruction that ravaged the island in 1450 B.C. was the work of just such an unexpected enemy: the Mycenaeans of mainland Greece.

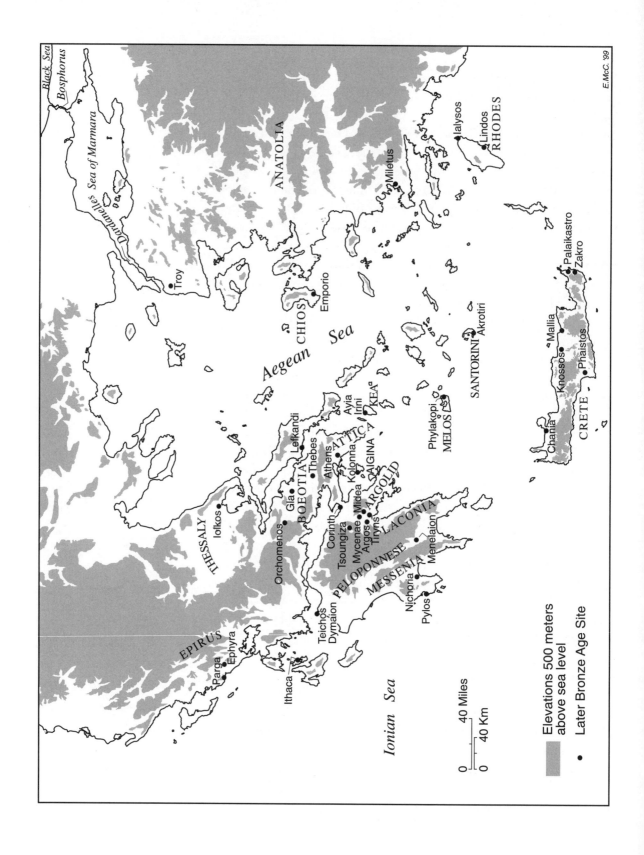

Black Sea

Bosphorus

Sea of Marmara

Dardanelles

ANATOLIA

Troy

Miletus

Ialysos
Lindos
RHODES

Emporio

CHIOS

Aegean Sea

Palaikastro
Zakro

SANTORINI
Akrotiri

Mallia

Phylakopi
MELOS

KEA

Ayia
Irini

Chania

Knossos

Phaistos

CRETE

Iolkos

THESSALY

Lefkandi

ATTICA

Orchomenos

Gla

BOEOTIA

Thebes

Athens

Kolonna

AIGINA

Corinth

Mycenae Midea

Tsoungiza Argos ARGOLID

Tiryns

LACONIA

Menelaion

PELOPONNESE

MESSENIA

Nichoria

Teichos
Dymaion

EPIRUS

Pylos

Parga

Ephyra

Ithaca

Ionian Sea

40 Miles

0   40 Km

Elevations 500 meters
above sea level

• Later Bronze Age Site

E.McC. '99

THE MYCENAEANS

The Mycenaean Greeks of the mainland created a large, sprawling, gaudy barbaric civilization in the Late Bronze Age (1600–1100 B.C.). Their first appearance was in the Minoan New Palace Period, although the high point of their civilization came between 1400–1250 B.C., when the Minoans were no more. At first confined to the narrow valleys of the Peloponnese, especially the Argolid, and around Navarino Bay in the southwest, they eventually took their easily recognizable culture north as far as the Chalkidiki, south into the islands, and east to the western portions of Asia Minor (for instance, to the newly discovered Mycenaean town of Miletus on the west coast of Anatolia). Their influence, if not the physical presence of the Mycenaeans, is felt also in Cyprus, the Levant, Egypt, North Africa, Sicily, Italy, Sardinia, and even in central Europe. Figure 4.28 shows the major Late Bronze Age sites.

Unlike the Minoans, who nevertheless had a considerable influence on Mycenaean material culture, the Mycenaeans were a Greek-speaking people. Their glyphic script, or Linear B, which was deciphered by the brilliant architect and linguist Michael Ventris in 1952, was used to write a dialect older than Homer by close to a thousand years, but recognizably Greek. Scholars have exercised considerable ingenuity in investigating the origins of these early Greeks, but so far a solution has eluded them. Are the Mycenaeans the descendants of an aboriginal people who trace their roots back to the beginning of the Neolithic period 9,000 years ago or even earlier? Or are they descendents of marauding intruders who appeared in the Early Bronze Age or even later, shortly before they began to write Greek on clay tablets? No one knows.

But Greeks they were, and the Mycenaean Empire (its most com-

4.28 *Opposite.* The locations of the principal sites of the Late Bronze Age. In the early phases of this period the Minoan palaces on Crete were still flourishing. After 1450 B.C. most were destroyed, leaving the Mycenaean sites on the mainland as the focus of continuing civilization. Note the continuing concentration of sites in east-central Greece, particularly in Boeotia and the Argolid. Large fortified settlements on the Cycladic islands, such as Phylakopi (Melos) and Kolonna (Aigina), have many unique features and were probably politically independent as well.

4.29 Fresco of flying fish from Phylakopi on Melos, an example of the unique island style of wall decoration.

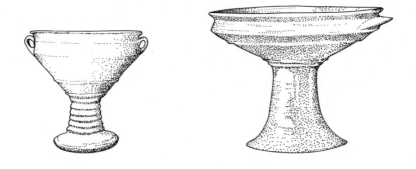

4.30 Two examples of Middle Helladic pottery, which was in use on the mainland at the beginning of the Mycenaean rise to power. These are drinking cups on a heroic scale, requiring two-handed drinking. The forms imitate metallic shapes and were painted silvery gray, burnished red, pale yellow, and black.

mon, if somewhat grandiloquent epithet) is a true high-Greek civilization with proto-urban communities, writing, a state religion, a large geographic territory, a centralized administration, and an organized military. The Mycenaean Empire was composed of many separate principalities, mini-kingdoms each based on a single easily defended citadel that commanded trade routes and a sizable piece of arable land.

Excavations and surveys in recent years have brought the number of known Mycenaean citadels to more than fifteen. Each principality was very small, rarely controlling a territory of more than about 1,000 square kilometers. A good example of the scale of the Mycenaean world is found in the southwestern Peloponnese. The kingdom controlled from the Palace of Nestor at Pylos near the modern town of Chora reached its largest extent in the fourteenth century B.C., when it embraced an area of 2,000 square kilometers (1,250 square miles); as such, the Pylian kingdom was one of the largest territories controlled from a single palace (see Figure 4.31). For purposes of comparison, note that the kingdom of Pylos was exactly the same size as the state of Rhode Island in the United States. All ancient polities were very small, probably because it was so difficult to establish and maintain communications and transportation on primitive road systems over even small distances. The Linear B tablets found in the Pylos palace archives tell us that this territory was nevertheless large enough to require division for purposes of administration into two provinces, which together included about 200 small towns and villages.

Our survey of their culture must first distinguish the ways in which the Mycenaeans differed from or were similar to the Minoans, who were their close geographic neighbors and had a well-established culture long before the emergence of the Mycenaeans on the mainland. The Mycenaean centers were palaces, which might at first glance seem to have been of Minoan inspiration. But the Mycenaean palaces no more resemble the Minoan ones than a Pershing tank resembles a Ferrari. The heart of the Mycenaean palace is a single room, the so-called megaron, with a central hearth, four surrounding columns, and a throne situated on the right side as one enters (see Figure 4.32). All the rest of the rooms, corridors, and dependencies were built around a central axis that knifes through the megaron. This symmetry was carefully planned by the architect. The approach to the megaron was controlled by passage through several small courtyards, each with its own columns. Smaller rooms attached to the courtyards held the palace archives of tablets and served other functions necessary to the palace. These central courtyards and the megaron were flanked by long corridors that led to storerooms for olive oil, wine, pottery, and other necessities. The palace flanks were composed of royal apartments, workshops for craftsmen, and additional storage rooms.

Smaller, more compact, and quite tightly focused on a single

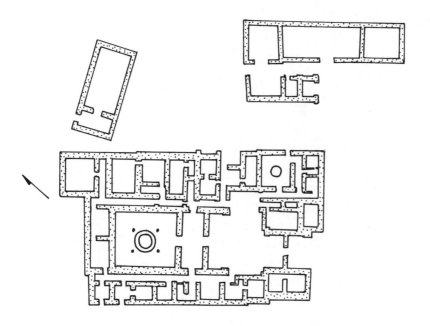

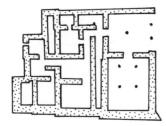

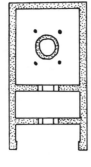

4.31 The Palace of Nestor at Pylos. This site is identified with Nestor, the elder statesman of Homer's poems. It was excavated by Carl Blegen of the University of Cincinnati, and the palace plan is the most complete that we have at our disposal. Note the firm central axis that runs from the one central entrance through a small courtyard and porch into the megaron, which is thought to be a throne room. The long corridors recall the plan of the House of the Tiles at Lerna and hark back to the Neolithic period. The surrounding rooms and outlying buildings are storerooms, workrooms, and living quarters. The building was at least two stories tall but also very small: the whole thing would fit in the central court at Knossos. A number of plans are available for Pylos and show different phases of the building's history. The plans are, frankly, not easily reconciled in their details, and the one shown here is a simplified version, an interpretation of the major outlines of the palace in its latest phase, ca. 1200 B.C., on the eve of its final destruction.

4.32 Plan of a typical Mycenaean megaron, the heart of the palace.

administrative function, the Mycenaean palace is both more easily comprehended by modern eyes and much duller than its distant Minoan cousin. Mycenaean palaces were also much smaller, even with upper stories. The typical Mycenaean palace would fit neatly in the central court of Knossos. Even the best-preserved Mycenaean palace is a poor thing architecturally. Only limited use was made of squared stone in the foundations. It was built almost completely of squat adobe brick. Rooms were small, square, and evidently airless. Plumbing was conspicuously rare—a bathtub at Pylos and a shower stall in Tiryns appear to have been afterthoughts. Lively wall paintings, and a profusion of colors on the plastered floors and door jambs livened things up a bit, but nowhere were the wide-open windows and doors, the alabaster dadoes (decorative facings on wall bases), and light wells of a properly fitted-out Minoan palace.

Mycenaean art elicits a grim fascination (see Figure 4.33). Frescoes depict dogs that worry boars while hunters close in; hirsute tribesmen dressed in skins are skewered by clean-shaven warriors; and chariots with stiffly upright women trundle past trees shaped like ping pong paddles. The Pylos throne-room paintings are the most coherent of the compositions, with griffins flanking the throne, a lyre-playing singer on a rock, and a riot of polychrome rosettes, wave patterns, spirals, and squirming octopi. These efforts to brighten up the place did not detract from the central purpose: administering the economic, political, religious, and social life of the kingdom.

The invaluable decipherment of Linear B, made possible by the discovery of an intact archive room at Pylos by the American archaeologist Carl Blegen in 1939 opens a window into the life of the palace. The political, economic, and religious aspects of Mycenaean society are reasonably well known. At the top of a rigorously hierarchical social pyramid was the king, known as the "wanax." The wanax ruled a small kingdom from his throne room. Each palace had a territory about the size of a modern administrative district or province in Greece today. Warriors, priests and priestesses, craftsmen, farmers, and slaves worked for and received allotments from the palace. Scented perfume based on olive oil, bronze weapons, jewelry, ivory knickknacks,

4.33 Mycenaean soldiers in full uniform from a painted vase of the last phase of Mycenaean power.

pottery (see Figure 4.34), and furniture were produced both in the palace and in dependent villages to be shipped abroad in exchange for gold, copper, tin, ivory, glass, wood, and incense. In one room of the Palace of Nestor at Pylos nearly 10,000 clay drinking cups were stored in stacks, and at Mycenae squat oil jars awaited filling with perfume. The tablets kept careful note of each transaction. The whole palace was an operation more like an old-fashioned Sears, Roebuck and Co. (or maybe upscale enough to be Harrod's) than the seat of a predatory warlord, which is otherwise the subject of the art (see Figure 4.35).

The commercial interest in perfume trade and an apparently keen interest in fine luxury goods such as ivory boxes and glass-paste jewelry did not prevent them from maintaining military appearances. Gold finger rings depict warriors in combat, and the kings were buried in shaft graves magnificently stuffed with bronze weapons decorated with gold, silver, and rock crystal, which even included full sets of body armor, chariots, and horses sacrificed to serve their masters on the battlefields of the afterlife (see Figures 4.36 and 4.37).

All this swagger was not for show alone. The weapons and military gear from many Mycenaean burials are grimly functional (see

4.34 Late Bronze Age spouted jugs.

4.35 Mycenaean(?) soldiers in full uniform from a wall painting in a house at Akrotiri on Santorini. The speckled rectangles are shields covered with cow hides, and the plumed helmets are plated with split boar's tusks.

4.36 These fabulous bronze daggers are the finest products of the Shaft Grave period (first phase of the Late Bronze Age). They are inlaid with silver and gold figures and had handles of precious materials (the preserved handle is gold) fastened to the blades with golden nails. These weapons were for display and were buried with high-ranking individuals.

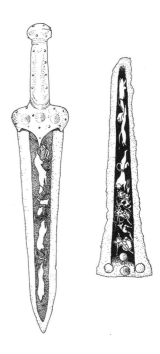

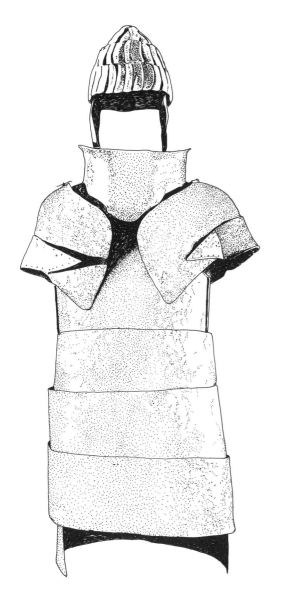

4.37 A complete set of bronze armor discovered in a large chamber tomb at Dendra (between Nafplion and Mycenae in the Argolid) and now in the Nafplion Archaeological Museum. The individual plates were strung together with leather straps to permit the free movement of the body, clear evidence that this armor was completely functional. The armor, together with the images of soldiers from artworks, gives us a clear impression of the professionalism of the Mycenaean warrior.

Figure 4.38). Short swords shaped like a butcher's cleavers, deadly spear points, and tough boar's-tusk helmets were clearly made to be used, and we can safely assume that even the most perfumed of Mycenaean kings was dangerous when roused. The legends of the Seven Against Thebes and the Trojan War, which we believe were inspired at least partly by real Bronze Age events, are evidence of the martial spirit of the Mycenaeans. And the blackened ruins of the last Minoan palaces are evidence of Mycenaean military efficiency.

On the spiritual life of the Mycenaeans we are on somewhat firmer ground than we were with the Minoans. The names of gods and goddesses dot the tablets. Of the approximately 30 gods and goddesses named, some are familiar from later Greek religion (such as Zeus, Hera, and Poseidon); others belong only to the archaic Greek religion of the Mycenaean world (such as Potnia Theron, "the mistress of the animals"). It is clear that the Mycenaeans worshiped a large pantheon of both male and female deities. The gods owned property, even slaves, and were worshiped in countryside shrines and in small cult rooms in

4.38 An ivory furniture inlay in the form of a Mycenaean warrior wearing a plumed helmet plated with split boar's tusks. These helmets are mentioned in Homer's poems, evidence that the later Greek world had some memory of the Mycenaean world.

4.39 Typical Mycenaean terra-cotta figurines. These figurines are a ubiquitous feature of any Mycenaean site, including settlements, shrines, and burials. They come in a variety of sizes and forms, but most represent females, often with upraised arms and wearing long skirts resembling, rather distantly, the fine faience figurine from Knossos in Fig. 4.25.

the palaces. Worship in caverns was rare, and true mountain-peak sanctuaries are found only occasionally (in the Argolid, for instance, and on the island of Aigina). It is disputed whether their wall art and large sculpture represent the deities, but the vast number of little clay figurines found in Mycenaean homes and graves (which now peer out of every museum case in the country) are no doubt connected to the everyday worship of the Mycenaean gods (see Figure 4.39).

The Mycenaean Empire and Its Culture

The Linear B tablet archives (see Figure 4.40) do not inform us about the relationship of the Mycenaean palaces with one another, but recently discovered Egyptian diplomatic records and Hittite archives from their capital of Hattusa at Boğazköy in Turkey clearly treat the Mycenaeans as an equal power, a force to be reckoned with in diplomacy and battle. Did they think of the Mycenaeans as a single polity with one overlord or as a cluster of statelets that were clumped together for convenience?

Because the scattered palaces are so similar in layout and material culture, right down to small details, the sway of Mycenaean influence and power can be likened to an empire in the way that historians use the term. Mycenaean commercial interests and relations stretched in time from one end of the Mediterranean to the other, far exceeding the reach of the Minoans, and put the Mycenaeans on an equal footing with their Near Eastern neighbors.

Despite the geographic extent of their activities, Mycenaean palaces

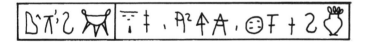

4.40 An example of Mycenaean Linear B script. This hieroglyphic writing was derived from Minoan Linear A and was used to keep records on clay tablets. An archive of such tablets was found at the Palace of Nestor at Pylos, and fragments have come from many other citadels, including many found in the Palace of Minos at Knossos. Linear B owes nothing to the contemporary cuneiform or hieroglyphics used in the Near East and Egypt; it may be more closely related to the still poorly understood notations seen on Neolithic "computers" and Early Bronze Age pots and seals.

are small affairs. Most were part of a citadel, a defensible eminence that in the later period had distinctive, heavy walls for fortification. Within the walls, dependencies consisted chiefly of large private houses clustered around the palace. Outside the walls there is often an extensive burial ground of chamber tombs and large domed sepulchers (*tholoi*) (see Figures 4.41, 4.42, and 4.43).

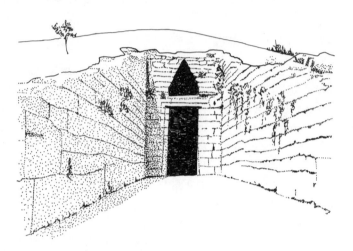

4.41   Facade of the Treasury of Atreus, the biggest and best-preserved tholos tomb at Mycenae. There are eight others at that site. This tomb dates to the end of the Bronze Age, ca. 1250 B.C., and represents that last and most glorious period of Mycenaean power. It was certainly a royal tomb, but it was plundered in antiquity and was already empty when visited by Pausanius in the second century A.D.

4.42   Cross section of the Treasury of Atreus. The beehive-shaped dome is thirteen meters high (a four-story building would fit inside), and the lintel block over the doorway weighs more than 100 tons. It is an engineering masterpiece. In our opinion it was designed by the master architect (or architects?) who executed the fortifications around Mycenae, Tiryns, Medea, and Gla. This Daedalus may have come from Anatolia, where Trojan and Hittite kings built similar fortifications.

Some of the citadels were linked by a system of superbly engineered roads and bridges. The remains of a network of small villages are seen in the countryside, the villages barely distinguishable in size or function from their Neolithic or Early Bronze Age counterparts except by the distinctive Mycenaean pottery. In the 1980s and 1990s, a survey of the Berbati Valley on which we collaborated revealed the existence of isolated farmhouses in the vicinity of Mycenae. The uniformly distributed hierarchical settlement is dull in contrast with the Minoans' more eclectic and dispersed mixture of villas, villages, and shrines.

Mycenaean citadels with their megaron palaces are more numerous than Minoan palaces. Depending on how liberally we apply the term "palace," more than fifteen are identifiable on the mainland, and more are suspected to exist. The citadel of Mycenae appears to modern eyes to be preeminent among the mainland palace sites, both because of its privileged position in Greek poetry and myth and because of solid archaeological evidence. Mycenae was the ancestral seat of the House of Atreus, whose exploits fueled the imaginations of later Greek playwrights. One of the last kings, Agamemnon, led the greatest of Greek armies against Troy according to an ancient and credible legend. Because of this legendary fame, Heinrich Schliemann began the excavations at Mycenae in 1876 that led to his spectacular discovery of the rich burials in the Shaft Grave Circle that form one of the greatest treasures of the National Archaeological Museum of Athens.

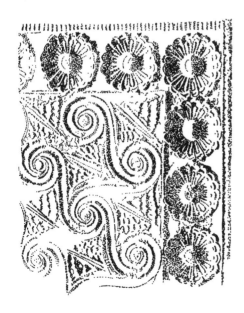

4.43   A fragment of the carved stone ceiling in a side room of a ruined tholos tomb at Orchomenos that hints at the rich interior decoration of these tombs.

The Shaft Grave Circle tombs belong to the earliest phase of Mycenaean civilization (Late Helladic in archaeological terms), yet they
seem to explode upon the scene without precedent. The tombs were
discovered by Schliemann directly within the fortification walls inside
a circular walled area (hence the designation "Shaft Grave Circle,"
which became Shaft Grave Circle A when a second circle was discovered). Six graves with the remains of nineteen people overflowed
with golden cups and jewelry, bronze weapons, silver and bronze
vases, and a profusion of other rich finds. The most memorable pieces
are weighty golden death masks that were placed over the faces of the
dead kings (see Figures 4.44 and 4.45). Letting enthusiasm race ahead

4.44   The best gold death mask from Shaft Grave Circle A excavated
by Heinrich Schliemann in August 1876. Thought at first to be the
image of Agamemnon himself, it belongs to an early Mycenaean king,
ca. 1600–1550 B.C. The practice of placing gold masks in richly
appointed graves of kings comes from Egypt, where the best-known
example is the mask of Tutankhamun.

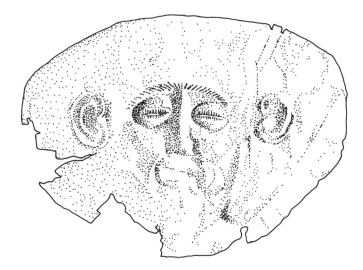

4.45 This gold death mask from Mycenae is a good example of the generally provincial quality of the early Mycenaean finds. For all their pretensions, the Mycenaeans were barbarians in comparison with their sophisticated neighbors in Crete, Troy, the Near East, and Egypt, the touchstone of civilization in the eastern Mediterranean world.

of the facts, Schliemann mistook the burials for those of Agamemnon and his followers. They are some 450 years too old for that, but they certainly attest to the barbarous swagger and dash of the early Mycenaean warrior princes.

Shaft Grave Circle B was discovered in the 1950s; although it is a good deal less spectacular than Shaft Grave Circle A, the graves there can be linked to the local Bronze Age settlements of the previous period. There is a significant chronological gap between the construction of Shaft Grave Circle B (the older of the two) and Shaft Grave Circle A sometime after 1600 B.C. and the period when the palace and walls that remain today were built. Almost all of the great palaces, with their accompanying fortifications, gateways, and monumental tombs, were built during the third and final phase of the culture (known as Late Helladic III among archaeologists) dating to ca. 1400–1100 B.C.

Apart from the palaces themselves, and the roads linking centers, the countryside was controlled with dams, canals, and terraces mighty in scope and professionally engineered. Some of them are still working today to control water runoff and slope erosion, having performed these functions with little or no maintenance for 3,000 years.

Impressive building projects were the fortification walls at sites such as Mycenae, Midea, Tiryns, Athens, and Gla (see Figure 4.46). Massive walls of "Cyclopean" masonry (rough blocks ascribed by the wondering ages to the mythical giants, the Cyclopes) surround key citadels and include a catalogue of up-to-date features required by Bronze Age military experts. The fortification walls, many of which are dilapidated but still standing, are tall and very thick, with towers to cover the small gateways, and even smaller postern gates or sally ports allowed for surprise raids on the enemy or escape. Inside the walls are deep rock-cut springs with hidden staircases to give access only to defenders.

But the most impressive building feats are the tholos tombs. There are nine of them at Mycenae and smaller numbers at most other sites. The Treasury of Atreus (a traditional name) at Mycenae is the most splendid of them all, and the best-preserved example. These tombs were surely for kings (Figures 4.41, 4.42, and 4.43).

There is no doubt that the fortifications were built to protect the citadels from an organized besieging army, not merely marauding coastal pirates. The Mycenaeans may have wanted to awe their neighbors and visiting dignitaries with these walls, but military experts have pronounced the Mycenaean walls efficient and fully functional defen-

4.46   The Lion Gate at Mycenae. Constructed along with the fortifications around 1250 B.C., this gateway controlled access to the citadel. The sculptured slab over the doorway represents two lions flanking a Minoan-style column. It is thought to represent the ruling house of Mycenae. It is one of the rare examples of monumental sculpture in the Aegean world before classical times.

sive barriers. The Mycenaeans may have been traders in times of peace and when it suited them, but the line between trader and raider is easily crossed. When they turned their minds to military affairs, they were very serious indeed. For the Mycenaeans' own view of their prowess as warriors, see Figure 4.47.

Turning from the monuments intended for public display, it is evident that the Mycenaean economy was based on the same simple mix of cereal farming and animal husbandry that had sustained all of the prehistoric cultures on the mainland since the beginning of the Neolithic period. The Linear B tablets (chiefly from the Pylos and Knossos archives) supply many details about the highly developed crafts in this period, which were probably produced in part as objects for trade and export. The tablets list imports such as amber (from the Baltic Sea region), metal (gold, silver, copper, and tin), dyestuffs, and spices (such as coriander). These imports were used, along with locally available materials, to develop a large variety of handicrafts intended for prac-

4.47 This fresco from the Palace of Nestor at Pylos depicts a fight between uniformed Mycenaean warriors and long-haired, skin–clad men otherwise unidentified. Does this scene depict an actual historical event? Or is it a scene from a myth? Whatever it is, the Mycenaeans' view of themselves is clear: they were well groomed, smartly dressed, heavily armed, and victorious over their "barbarian" opponents.

tical use and the international market in luxury items. The tablets list bronze smiths (nearly 400 in the Pylos region alone), ivory workers, goldsmiths, chariot makers, flax weavers, textile makers (the tablets from Mycenaean Knossos list sheep in the tens of thousands), potters, and many other craft workers. The leading exports from Pylos included linen cloth, woolen textiles, bronze, and perfume, as well as lesser amounts of wine, hides, leather, and jewelry.

The perfume trade is particularly interesting. The Mycenaeans evidently used olive oil (probably from the wild olive) in the production of perfume scented with coriander, rose, and other spices and flowers, which was exported around the Mediterranean from Sicily to Palestine. The long-distance perfume trade can be traced through discoveries of the distinctive and easily recognized ceramic containers called stirrup jars (because of the shape of the pouring spout) used to transport it (see Figure 4.48).

The large number of clay drinking cups found on all Mycenaean sites betrays a serious interest in wine. The textiles mentioned in the tablets have been lost, but there is much existing physical evidence of the skilled bronze work, particularly in the form of weapons and armor. Corselets, greaves, shields, helmets, swords in great variety, daggers, spears, and archery equipment were made by expert craftsmen who used large quantities of bronze in their construction. Some of the weaponry was for combat, but many pieces were purely for show. One thinks here especially of the inlaid daggers found in the shaft graves at Mycenae (Figure 4.36). Particular attention was given to the production of fine-quality luxury goods. Small boxes and sculptures of ivory manufactured from elephant tusks and hippopotamus incisors imported from Syria abound, and much ivory was cut and carved for inlays to adorn wooden furniture (Figure 4.38). There was also a line of blue glass-paste jewelry made from Syrian glass ingots, which is a signature of Mycenaean craftwork.

Although the luxury objects and the military hardware grab the viewer's attention in museums, the humble productions of the Mycenaean potters remain the best-known and most easily recognized ar-

4.48 Typical Mycenaean pottery. *Top*, a two-handled drinking goblet called a kylix. *Bottom*, a stirrup jar with an offset spout used for transporting perfumed olive oil, a major export product of the Mycenaean Empire.

tifacts from the Late Bronze Age. Mycenaean pots are durable and lustrous, if not very colorful. Perky, thin-stemmed wine goblets and big mixing bowls for wine were favorite products. The pots were thrown on the potter's wheel, have very thin walls, and are well fired and hard. A uniform yellowish brown color, Mycenaean ceramics are decorated with dark reddish brown painted designs that range from abstract floral elements to lively scenes of chariot races and other heroic exploits. Large-scale painted scenes of chariot races and combat appear on the bigger bowls, called kraters, which were used, it is presumed, for mixing wine with water and were thus prominently displayed at large gatherings. One outstanding example of a painted krater is the Warrior Vase found by Schliemann from the twilight period of Mycenae. Lines of heavily armed soldiers march across the belly of the bowl while a maiden cheers them on from under a handle (Figure 4.33). The troops have a certain rustic look to them, but one cannot help recalling the many poignant leave-taking scenes in Homer's poetry, and we suspect that many a tear may have been splashed in the wine taken from this rather special mixing bowl.

The Destruction of the Mycenaeans

Myths of the Heroic Age from Homer to Hesiod are replete with tales of war: the Seven Against Thebes; the first siege of Troy by Herakles; the Second Trojan War of Agamemnon, Achilles, Odysseus, and Hektor; and the Return of the Sons of Herakles. Even without these myths of dubious historicity we would still suspect that the winds of war blew down the walls of the Mycenaean citadels.

Beginning late in the last period of greatness known as Late Helladic IIIB, the signs of war and preparations for war are everywhere to be seen. The great fortified walls surrounding the citadels of Mycenae, Tiryns, Midea, Athens, Gla, and other sites stand out. They were built in the last period of Mycenaean civilization. Some had secret springs accessed by hidden tunnels, and massive gateways were built to control the flow of traffic to the palaces on the citadels. Granaries and vaults to store supplies sprang up like mushrooms, sometimes built right into the fabric of the walls, as can be seen at Tiryns (see Figure 4.49). While some scholars have pointed to the many features of the redesigned citadels that were clearly for show rather than military utility (such as the Lion Gate at Mycenae, Figure 4.46), the hefty functionality of the 50-foot-thick walls speaks for itself (see

Figure 4.50). The military engineers who designed these fortresses were experienced and may well have come from Hittite Anatolia, where there are similar, and older, walls. These engineers built the walls to repel real enemies in real wars.

But it was all to no avail. Archaeological strata and site catalogues reveal that a steady wave of destruction and abandonment swept through the mainland Greek world starting around 1200 B.C. and affected between 60 and 100 major sites, and probably many hundreds of small villages, hamlets, and farmsteads that have yet to be inventoried. The destruction continued off and on for a hundred years or more. Some sites were destroyed early and never recovered (Thebes), while others recovered virtually completely for one or two generations before finally being obliterated (Mycenae). Very few escaped altogether, and no more than two or three sites (such as Athens) survived the final wave of destructions around 1100 B.C. to continue into the early Iron Age more or less intact.

Elsewhere the destruction was complete. From 1979 to 1991 we codirected survey projects in the Argolid, the acknowledged center of Mycenaean civilization. Teams of archaeologists trained to identify the smallest fragments of cultural material did closely spaced field walking to see if we could locate any small sites in the back country that survived the fall of the palatial citadels. Despite years of careful searching we found no sites at all that dated to the centuries immediately following the Mycenaean collapse (1100–950 B.C.).

For example, the survey in the Berbati Valley fell entirely within a fifteen-kilometer radius of Mycenae itself, and yet we could not find a single artifact dating to the period after the fall. Whatever the cause

4.49   Storage vaults built into the interior of the massive fortification walls at the citadel of Tiryns near Nafplion. These rooms stored provisions for resisting prolonged sieges.

4.50 The thirteenth-century B.C. fortification walls at Tiryns (and other Mycenaean citadels) were built of enormous, minimally worked stone blocks so large that the classical Greeks called the walls Cyclopean, believing that only the mythical Cyclopes giants could have built them. These magnificent walls, although reconstructed in part since the 1950s, testify to the engineering abilities of the Late Bronze Age peoples and the very real military threat perceived by the Mycenaeans in their last days.

of the Mycenaean catastrophe, the effects were awesome. It is certain that large portions of the Greek countryside were deserted, or at least so thinly populated that the inhabitants cannot be detected.

The implications are sobering. Later civilizations were large and flexible enough to withstand economic collapse or environmental disaster and survive, but the Mycenaean civilization vanished completely, and with it the entire surviving inventory of the Bronze Age Aegean heritage handed down from Helladic/Cycladic times and the Minoan world. Everything was lost—palace architecture, wall painting, fine pottery, glass technology, bronze metallurgy, and even writing itself. The later Hellenic civilization of classical times had to start over from scratch.

Today we believe that civilization will survive such catastrophes, but the fate of the Mycenaeans should give us pause for thought. And they were not alone. The Hittites were swept away at the end of the Bronze Age, and so were Troy and the Near Eastern state called Mitanni. Even the Egyptian state of Pharaoh Ramesses III teetered and nearly collapsed. The facts of the archaeological record have forced us to conclude that cultures can, and do, die.

CHAPTER FIVE

THE END OF THE
BRONZE AGE WORLD

The Mycenaean Empire was both cosmopolitan and glamorous, if rather unsophisticated. Judged by the only available standards, namely longevity and geographical spread, the Mycenaeans were the most successful of the Greek Bronze Age cultures. For more than 500 years they dominated the Aegean, waging war against their neighbors and trading with distant realms. Firmly rooted in the southern Greek mainland, they were able to extend their influence northward to establish themselves in Epirus, Thessaly, and Macedonia. Their trade with the Balkans and central Europe brought them into contact with cultures even less developed than their own. The Mycenaeans founded communities in the eastern Mediterranean on the islands of Crete, Rhodes, and Cyprus. They had settlements on the coast of Asia Minor and, perhaps as merchants or mercenary warriors, had their place in native towns along the Syro-Palestinian coast all the way to Egypt. Far to the west, Mycenaeans made their presence felt in Italy, Sicily, Sardinia, and even in distant Spain. A similar geographic spread of Greek-speaking peoples would not been seen again until the eighth century B.C.

Rough-edged and aggressive, trading and raiding in turn, the Mycenaean Greeks made themselves the political equals (in diplomatic terms) of the great states of Egypt and the Hittites, although these states had more land, greater material resources, and longer histories. The Mycenaeans earned a place at the table of world powers, rising from little adobe villages in the rocky Peloponnese to address the Egyptian god-king, Pharaoh, and the Hittite Great King as "brother." But such success incurs the wrath of heaven, and the Mycenaean palaces collapsed in a tidal wave of abandonments and fiery destructions that swept across the Aegean around 1200 B.C. and after. A few centers, including Mycenae itself, recovered for a time, but never reached the same level of cultural development, and these last centers were destroyed in turn by 1100 B.C., bringing the Bronze Age civilizations to a decisive end.

The collapse of Mycenaean civilization was not an isolated occurrence. The wave of destruction continued around the rim of the eastern Mediterranean, bringing down the Hittites in Asia Minor, the Mitanni, and other states in the Middle East and finally broke upon the delta of the Nile. The Egyptian state in the time of Ramesses III in the twentieth dynasty (namesake of the more famous Ramesses the Great in the nineteenth dynasty) resisted repeated attacks by land and sea made by the ever-mysterious Sea Peoples. The Pharaoh was successful, the Sea Peoples were driven off or taken prisoner, and Egypt alone of all the great Bronze Age states survived. The bas-relief sculptures and hieroglyphic texts on the monument of Medinet Habu describe the Egyptian victories and constitute one of the few surviving records of the upheavals that rocked the Mediterranean world at this time.

THE COLLAPSE OF A CIVILIZATION

The collapse of great established civilizations has always excited enormous archaeological interest. If the Minoan destructions can be ascribed to earthquake, volcanic eruption, or Mycenaean predation, what wave of destructions succeeded in bringing an entire age to an end? In this section we review the explanations that have been offered by archaeologists in recent years, though we find none of them to be completely satisfying. Archaeology may be able to reconstruct prehistoric cultures from their material remains, but the science is less successful at producing widely accepted theories for either the origins or the collapse of ancient societies. It may be impossible to fully explain a historical event that by its nature happened only once. With that in mind, we have nevertheless weighed the available explanations carefully and feel confident that we can at least eliminate the most improbable of them.

A CATALOGUE OF DISASTERS

Natural calamities have been invoked since ancient times to explain some of the destructions that overtook the Mycenaeans. Plato and Aristotle drew attention to dramatic changes in the Greek landscape that they attributed, at least in part, to changes in climate. In passages that are receiving new attention, these philosophers noted changes in forest cover and the distribution of surface water in Attica and the Argive Plain, both areas of importance in the Mycenaean period. Aristotle, in particular, claimed that in the area of Mycenae the fertility of the soil in the Argive Plain declined from the time of the Trojan War to his own day. Although he describes the changes in hydrology and fertility, he does not clearly explain the causes of these changes.

In recent times, scholars have searched the writings of Plato, Aristotle, and other ancient writers for clues to changes in the climate and environment that may have affected the development and even the survival of ancient civilizations. The leader of this movement was Rhys Carpenter, an American archaeologist and art historian who in 1968 made an influential case for drought as the cause of Mycenaean collapse. Relying on circumstantial evidence, chiefly the cycles of drought known from historic times and the spotty records of Mycenaean migrations and site abandonment, Carpenter painted a picture of crop failure, disease, revolution, and migration triggered by the delay or failure of seasonal rains. His account is plausible, as anyone familiar with the drought-stricken countries of the modern world can attest, but was unfortunately not supported by any direct evidence. Spurred on by this provocative study, climatologists, archaeologists, and historians have attempted to put the Carpenter hypothesis to the test. The consensus after 30 years, however, is a resounding, definitive "we don't know."

Scientists need several kinds of evidence. A drought at the end of the Bronze Age should be detectable in the records of vegetation found in pollen samples taken from bogs, lakes, and other places where pollen collects and survives for analysis. Long core samples taken from wetlands in mainland Greece and intended to retrieve sediments with ancient pollen have failed to show the usual effects of a drought. Tree pollen, for instance, normally declines in periods of drought, and over time trees are replaced by drought-resistant grasses and shrubs. This did not happen at the end of the Bronze Age. Other effects of drought, if there was one, such as crop failure and increase in disease among stressed populations, left no direct record. Mass graves, or evidence in human remains of stress from malnutrition, have yet to be discovered. Of course, say Carpenter's supporters, a drought of a few years would not be likely to leave a signature in the archaeological record that would survive more than 3,000 years. And yet, they argue, a two- or three-year drought would cause crops to fail, crippling a delicately balanced palace economy in a world without the physical means to transport bulky foodstuffs over long distances. A catastrophe such as this would have had a great impact on ancient cultures and would leave barely a physical trace, especially if the starving peasants had chosen flight or migration rather than slow death in the homeland. Such arguments are, unfortunately, unanswerable, and the search continues for definitive proof.

Another possibility is that floods and earthquakes together unsettled the Bronze Age world. Eberhard Zangger, a geoarchaeologist in Switzerland, has explored the combined geological and archaeological evidence for such forces in the Late Bronze Age. One compelling example for Zangger is Tiryns, in the Greek Argolid, where he discovered evidence of a massive flood that buried part of the settlement near the end of the period of greatest Mycenaean power. Other evidence comes from Troy in northwestern Turkey. Traditionally, Troy VIIa (the seventh settlement at the site) was regarded as the city sacked by Homer's Greeks, but many archaeologists now consider the highly developed settlement of Troy VI (the sixth settlement) as most likely to have been Homer's Troy. (Schliemann found nine superimposed settlements at the site of Hisarlik in Turkey, which he numbered I to IX from the bottom up.) Putting aside the question of whether Troy VI or VIIa was the Homeric city, Zangger argues that Troy VI was brought down by a catastrophic earthquake at roughly the same time that the flood was devastating Tiryns. Despite Zangger's persuasive arguments and the persistent claims of many archaeologists that there is evidence of earthquake damage at many Late Bronze Age sites, the cases are too isolated to be convincing as a *general* cause of cultural collapse. It should be noted that life went on at Tiryns and Troy and many other sites, and this is the natural tendency of any civilization struck with natural disaster: to recover what was lost and to carry on with the work of civilization.

A more dramatic explanation for the end of the Bronze Age invokes a different sort of natural disaster: the eruption of the great volcano on the Cycladic island of Santorini. Scientists agree that the so-called Minoan eruption of Santorini was the most powerful in the eastern Mediterranean in the past 20,000 years. Santorini is part of the South Aegean arc of volcanoes, which owe their origin to the colliding tectonic plates of Africa and Europe. It has erupted many times, but the Minoan eruption in the Late Bronze Age is one of the largest eruptions ever. It is estimated that the Santorini eruption resulted in the ejection of some 30 cubic kilometers of magma. By contrast, Mount Saint Helens in 1980 ejected 0.35 cubic kilometers, Mount Pinatubo in 1991 ejected five cubic kilometers, and even the famous eruption of Krakatoa in Indonesia in 1883 resulted in only ten cubic kilometers of ejecta. By any measure, the Minoan eruption of Santorini was a whopper.

One early use of this eruption to explain the collapse of a civilization was attempted by the amateur archaeologist Leon Pomerance, who argued that Santorini was destroyed by fire and water. Pomerance believed that the Minoan eruption of the Santorini volcano occurred in two stages: first the actual eruption, which took place around 1450 B.C. and was responsible for the seismic shocks and devastating fires that swept away the Minoan palaces on Crete; and second, the collapse of the exhausted volcanic cone close to 1200 B.C. That final collapse, he said, generated awesome tsunamis (tidal waves) that swept outward in expanding circles, destroying the harbors and fleets of the Mycenaean centers and wreaking the delicate and weakened Mycenaean societies in a single burst.

As the geologic study of the Minoan eruption of Santorini progressed, it became abundantly clear that there had been only one very large eruption. This undisputed fact encouraged other authors, such as Galanopoulos and Bacon, to invoke the destructive power of the eruption to explain the disruptions that brought an end to the Bronze Age Aegean world. They catalogued the disastrous effects of eruptions, itemizing the tsunamis, earthquakes, ash falls, blocked sunlight, and clouds of poisonous gases that must have wreaked havoc on the fragile shipping and agricultural infrastructure of the Minoans and Mycenaeans. Certainly, they argued, an eruption of such magnitude must have devastated surrounding cultures. This line of speculation had many followers, and it seemed for a while that the Minoan eruption of Santorini provided the *deus ex machina* to bring down the curtain on the Late Bronze Age Mediterranean world.

All of these arguments, unfortunately, are unconvincing. Since the discovery of the Minoan eruption there has been a long-term international effort by geologists to study it. The authorities agree that the eruption and collapse were a single event that occurred in either the sixteenth or seventeenth century B.C., too early to have played any part in the final destruction of either the Minoan or the Mycenaean world. Since the discovery of the buried city of Akrotiri on Santorini in 1968, the most striking conclusion is that the Minoan eruption had no discernible effect on Bronze Age Aegean civilizations. As we argue in more detail below, the eruption occurred too early, closer to 1628 B.C. to have had a hand in the Bronze Age catastrophe of 1200 B.C. Although this conclusion is in itself interesting, it is clear that the Minoan eruption of Santorini played no part in bringing about the end of the Bronze Age.

Princeton classicist Robert Drews has recently reviewed all the available theories about the Mycenaean collapse in an effort to explain what he terms the Catastrophe (with a capital C) that overwhelmed the Mediterranean civilizations at the end of the Bronze Age. We find ourselves convinced by Drews's carefully considered conclusion that none of the hypotheses of natural disaster adequately explains the catastrophe because their effects were generally local. Drought, flooding, earthquakes, and volcanic eruptions, for which decisive evidence is lacking in any case, could not cause destructions on a scale sufficiently large to account for the death of empires. The Mycenaean collapse was part of a widespread eastern Mediterranean disaster that destroyed many of the leading civilizations. If natural disasters were to blame, we would be mystified. History teaches us that empires may be shaken by natural disasters, but cultures, in the broadest sense of that term, struggle back into existence after earthquakes and floods. In the teeth of a natural disaster, the expected response is to rebuild, not to lie down and die. The Mycenaeans, in stark contrast, never recovered. The palaces, jewelry, wall painting, writing, even the Mycenaean style of painted pottery—all were lost or at least changed so much as to be unrecognizable.

For two centuries after the fall of the Mycenaeans there is no evidence of their distinctive material culture, and there is but scant evidence of human occupation in the old heartland. With few exceptions, most regions of the mainland were deserted or so thinly occupied that only traces of human presence are detectable in the archaeological record. Two or perhaps three sites survived the fall of the Mycenaeans into the Dark Age of 1100–950 B.C. Lefkandi in Euboia and Nichoria in the southwestern Peloponnese are the best known. It is perhaps significant that they were located on the edges of the Mycenaean kingdoms and were regional outliers rather than central places. A more typical history of the old Mycenaean kingdoms can be pieced together from archaeological surveys carried out in the 1980s and 1990s. These surveys were made in the Nemea Valley, the southern Argolid, and the Berbati and Limnes Valleys, all of which are within sight of Mycenae itself, and collectively they produced no evidence of human occupation in the Dark Age.

The Argolid was possibly the most densely populated of the Mycenaean kingdoms, and the richness of the excavated Late Bronze Age sites in this region appears to bear out the claims by poets and playwrights from the time of Homer (ca. 725 B.C.) that Mycenae was preeminent as the head of the Mycenaean world. The empty Argive landscape in the Dark Age tells us more about the scale of the Late Bronze Age catastrophe than the small settlements that managed to survive far from the centers of power.

The staggering scale of the disaster that overtook the Mycenaeans and expunged their culture cannot be explained by one or even many natural disasters. It was so comprehensive that the memory of the Mycenaeans appears to have been nearly wiped out. For millennia songs about Mycenaean heroes lingered on, but their history was imperfectly known and shot through with anachronisms. Scholars are convinced that even Homer's great epic poems, which appear to be wholly about the world of the Mycenaeans, tell more about Homer's own world of the Early Iron Age.

This cultural amnesia remained unexplored and unquestioned for nearly three millennia and only began to dissipate when Heinrich Schliemann's dramatic archaeological discoveries brought the Mycenaeans and the Bronze Age world back to the light of day. Looking back at the Late Bronze Age world after a century of scientific excavation and survey, we remain unconvinced that natural causes brought about its end. In our view an explanation for the catastrophe must be sought in the realm of human affairs, for history has taught us that human agency is most often responsible for the ruin of empires.

RUMORS OF WAR

The ancient Greeks were united in their acceptance of a tradition that was hoary with age by the time it reached Thucydides and that attributed the end of the Heroic Age (the Bronze Age in contemporary terms) to a great war with Troy. The Trojan War exhausted the physical resources of the Mycenaean palaces, laid waste the citadels and commercial emporia around the Aegean, and decimated the manpower of the Greek-speaking world. The Odyssey of Homer hints at these problems in tales of princes returning home from Troy to find rebellion, disorder, and riot. The myths connected with the House of Atreus at Mycenae, with their tragic saga of Agamemnon's return and death at the hands of his queen, Klytemnestra, help to flesh out the picture. Ancient historians from Herodotus to Thucydides relied of course on the testimony of the singers of songs, who related a clear tale of cause and effect between the event of the Trojan War and the fall of the Mycenaean Empire.

A complicating factor in the traditional account is the so-called Dorian Invasion, which we are told took place within a generation after the end of the Trojan War. Led by the Heraklids or "Sons of Herakles," the Dorians invaded the Peloponnese and attacked the citadels of the Mycenaeans, who were weakened and demoralized at home by their Pyrrhic victory at Troy. If the Dorians, presumably partly Mycenaeanized Greeks from central Greece, did not destroy the Mycenaeans themselves, as historians have surmised, then they were instrumental in hastening the decline that began with the overly ambitious and long Trojan War. This traditional two-part explanation of the Mycenaean failure and defeat is plausible, and it was accepted for more than 2,000 years as the best explanation for the collapse of the Late Bronze Age civilizations.

The traditional story of the Trojan War and the Dorian Invasion was accepted well into the twentieth century and can be found in school books and even some serious historical works today. It has nevertheless been seriously questioned by a generation of skeptical historians over the past 50 years after postwar archaeologists failed to produce any concrete support for the traditional explanation. Careful excavation at Mycenaean citadels, cemeteries, and smaller sites in the decades since the 1950s turned up very few artifacts or other cultural features that can be confidently attributed to the legendary Dorians. If the Dorians had invaded, for instance, archaeologists would have expected to find that their culture replaced the Mycenaean material culture at the beginning of the Iron Age beginning around 1100–1050 B.C. A decisive break in the archaeological record, however, does not occur. Iron tools and weapons, which were once thought to be evidence of the Dorians, were known before the end of the Bronze Age, and bronze implements continued in use well into the Iron Age. Although there is some evidence that the frequency of cremation increased and that the spectacular tholos tombs were abandoned in favor of more modest chamber tombs, excavators believe the transformation in mortuary customs was gradual rather than abrupt. Perhaps more to the point, there was no uniform change in the types of arms or the styles of painted pottery, jewelry, or dress that can be attributed to a single group of people who could reasonably be termed "Dorians."

An archaeological survey in the region of Douris (the reputed homeland of the Dorians in central Greece) was carried out in the 1970s in what may be seen as a desperate attempt to find archaeological evidence that a Dorian culture existed. But even this effort failed to detect the presence of a population numerous enough to have posed a military threat to the presumably disorganized and weakened Mycenaeans.

A further blow to the traditional model came when the American archaeologist Carl Blegen began excavations at Troy in the 1930s. The new excavations cast doubt on the other part of the received tradition, the Trojan War itself. Blegen believed that pottery evidence pointed to the shabby seventh settlement (VIIa) rather than the more substantial settlement of Troy VI as the "Homeric" city that was besieged by a Mycenaean army (cross-dating of pottery was the only means at the time to achieve a relative dating of sites in the Bronze Age). If Blegen is correct, Troy VIIa is too small, too poor, and simply too pathetic to have been the object of the greatest war known to the Greeks before the Peloponnesian war of the fifth century B.C. Blegen felt compelled to downgrade the Trojan War to the status of a minor raid on the coast of Asia Minor by a small group of Greeks, perhaps resulting from a tawdry trade dispute connected with the Black Sea traffic via the Dardanelles to the Aegean.

Does modern archaeological excavation and historical scholarship seem poised to sweep away once and for all the traditional explanation for the end of the Bronze Age? Is the only alternative one of the scenarios of natural disaster described above? Are humans to be absolved from any complicity in this historical disaster? Our preference for war as an explanation is in accord with Robert Drews's provocative but well-argued military explanation for the Bronze Age catastrophe. Drews first rejects natural disasters, as we noted before, as well as the complicated explanations generally called "systems collapse" that are favored by some social scientists. Systems-collapse models suggest that disruptions of trade or another activity set in motion a cascading collapse of the cultural and political infrastructure pushed by mechanisms of negative feedback. But systems-collapse models are unsatisfactory because they are really only elaborate *descriptions* of how the snowball effect of feedback works on cultural systems, rather than explanations of actual historical events.

In essence, Drews blames the Bronze Age catastrophe on large armed infantry forces, originally mercenary auxiliary troops, that emerged from the fringes of the civilized Mediterranean states. The new infantry, perhaps now acting under their own leaders, defeated the small professional corps of Late Bronze Age chariot warriors and was able to sack cities more or less at will. In short, the catastrophe was the result of an innovation in warfare that shifted the balance of power from the chariot-based military forces of the established states into the hands of former mercenary infantries who used javelins and long swords to mow down their former masters.

This short summary of Drews's argument does not do full justice to the hypothesis, and not all scholars accept his evidence or his conclusions. But in our opinion Drews's explanation is the best one going, if for no other reason than that it offers a testable explanation grounded in historical context and understandable in human terms. Although the military revolution he describes is not closely dated, it seems to have occurred around the pivotal year of 1200 B.C., quite close to the long-held traditional date for the Trojan War, and this fact strengthens our belief that the Trojan War must have been as significant as the ancient historians always insisted that it was.

We think that the Trojan War was likely one of the defining events that set in motion the military revolution described by Drews, which snowballed into the catastrophe that closed the Bronze Age. Troy VI was evidently large, rich, and surrounded by powerful fortifications, and new German excavations have shown that Troy VI was larger than Schliemann or his colleague Wilhelm Dörpfeld, who excavated at Troy after Schliemann's death, ever imagined. With a stronghold at the mouth of the Dardanelles, the Trojans controlled one of the vital chokepoints in maritime commerce between the Mediterranean and the Black Sea with all the lands that lay around it. Despite her power and success, Troy VI was destroyed, perhaps after a long siege and bitter fighting. Contrary to the revision of the evidence carried out by

Blegen, it is clear from the recovered remains that a conflagration destroyed Troy VI in its final phase, and weapons and scattered human remains were recovered by the early excavators from the charred ruins.

What are we to make of the strong fortifications around many of the Mycenaean citadels, especially in the Argolid? Excavations in the 1960s determined that the most famous of these walls at Mycenae and Tiryns were erected about 1250 B.C., close to the time of the destruction of Troy VI. Elaborate preparations for sieges have also been detected at Tiryns, Mycenae, Medea, Athens, and Gla, and include storehouses, secret springs accessible only from within the citadel, and postern gates for sallies. These late works, it can be argued, are evidence that the Mycenaeans feared military attack from an enemy powerful enough to mount a sustained siege.

But what possible enemy existed whose activities were widespread enough to include the entire Aegean world in its scope? According to Drews, the new mercenary infantry corps were the culprits, and they are perhaps connected with the rather mysterious "Sea Peoples." The Sea Peoples have been nominated by many authorities, including Drews, as agents of Mycenaean destruction. They are known from some historical documents to have ravaged the eastern Mediterranean littoral and migrated to the Levant and ultimately Egypt, where they were defeated by Ramesses III, whose victory monument at Medinet Habu (which depicts the battles between the Egyptians and the Sea Peoples) is perhaps the best evidence for the importance of the invaders who attacked Egypt by sea and by land.

Although the Sea Peoples are intriguing protagonists in the drama of Bronze Age catastrophes, intensive research has failed to turn up any evidence that they or Drews's other mercenaries were active on the Greek mainland, and the hypothesis that outside invaders destroyed the Mycenaean civilization remains unproven.

Historical cataclysms can never be reduced to a single cause, and even in our own times, global events from the world wars to the collapse of communism defy summary explanation. It would be presumptuous of archaeologists to hazard a single explanation for the catastrophe or catastrophes that brought the Bronze Age to an end, but it is nevertheless possible to speculate on plausible causes.

In this context, we think it is time to seriously consider the belief, professed since ancient times, that the Trojan War played a major role in the collapse of Mycenaean civilization. This traditional explanation should not be dismissed simply because it is old. It has, after all, the weight of authority: the people closest to the time and question believed it, as did the descendants of the people who were involved. Perhaps they also had access to sources of knowledge, such as songs, poems, or sagas that are now lost?

A new archaeological expedition to Troy under the direction of Manfred Korfmann of the University of Tübingen that began in 1988 has uncovered new evidence supporting the long-held view that Troy VI is the best candidate for Homer's city. Its vast walls and solid monumental buildings, along with a newly discovered lower city, itself evidently surrounded by a defensive ditch encompassing an area four times as large as the citadel first explored by Schliemann, are evidence that Troy was a formidable Bronze Age power and a worthy target for a large-scale Greek expedition.

On the mainland, the Mycenaean citadels were fortified only shortly before the traditional date for the siege of Troy (in ancient Greek reckoning, 1184 B.C.; ca. 1250 B.C. in modern terms). Walls like those of Tiryns, Mycenae, and Gla were not standard features of the older citadels, but were built in a short period of time and to the exacting standards of experienced military engineers. Although they were useful propaganda for Mycenaean power, they are also clearly intended to function defensively, particularly against prolonged sieges. Some authorities have noted the similarity of the walls around the Mycenaean citadels and walls in Anatolia (at Hattusa for instance, the capital of the Hittites) and not least at Troy VI itself. They recall to mind the imitative arms buildup by states in later historical periods as tensions rose before the actual outbreak of hostility and all-out war.

The great labor and expense lavished upon the military facilities at the traditional Homeric centers of conflict from Mycenae to Troy have all the hallmarks of preparations for a major war. According to traditional accounts, the victorious Greeks exhausted themselves in this war, and in its aftermath the great centers fell apart, opening the door to raids, though perhaps not permanent settlement, by armed bands from the northern frontiers. These raiders, perhaps the loose groups of infantry envisioned by Robert Drews, perhaps with no clear leader, were later lumped together as "Dorians." They came from the frontiers of the Mycenaean world, but many aspects of their culture did not differ substantially from the palace-based culture of the principal kingdoms. There was a temporary revival of some centers after the first wave of destruction in 1200 B.C.—for instance, at Mycenae itself—which lasted for as much as a century. Could these surviving centers have been in the hands of dynasts or leaders who thought of themselves as Dorians? Perhaps ruled by successive waves of adventurers and plunderers who filtered down from the northern marches to probe the failing defenses of the last kingdoms? We shall never be certain, but the outcome was ensured: once the balanced system of Mycenaean society and economy was disrupted and the shipping and trade lines were broken, the entire civilization tottered on its foundation. The kingdoms were too tightly controlled by the palaces to survive their destruction, and once the centers were destroyed or abandoned the entire machinery of the state ground to a halt.

But what happened to the Mycenaean population, the people themselves? The lower orders, particularly farmers and slaves, may have remained in their villages as long as possible, but as things got worse in the chaos following the Trojan War they may have joined bands of "Dorians" or retreated to secluded areas. This might also account for the signs of continuity observed at a few sites in the Peloponnese and Euboia, or for the survival of simplified forms of Mycenaean material culture into the Iron Age. The upper classes, including the princes and senior warriors who resided in the great houses inside the walled citadels, may have emigrated in small groups, perhaps taking to piracy or joining Drews's mercenary infantry (or the Sea Peoples) to exploit the collapse of order.

Some sober-minded scholars have seen expatriate Mycenaean warriors among the Sea Peoples who raided Cyprus, the Levant, and Egypt at the end of the Bronze Age. The Sea Peoples may have been a group of professional warriors and their dependents from states around the Aegean world who joined their former tormenters. It has even been suggested that displaced Mycenaeans became the Philistines when they occupied Palestine (both names derived from Peleset, the Egyptian name of one group of Sea Peoples) after the defeat of the Sea Peoples in the Nile delta by Ramesses III.

It may seem strange that Mycenaean Greeks ended their days in Palestine facing off with the ancient Israelites. But it is no stranger, we suppose, than Vandals of Scandinavian origin fighting their way in the fifth century of our era across central and western Europe, through Spain, to establish a kingdom in northern Africa that would endure for more than a century. Yet the strange tale of Vandalic migrations and success is an established historical fact, even if the plot would be considered too improbable for a work of fiction. The historical realities of the Vandals and perhaps the Sea Peoples are thus examples of the unexpected twists and nearly unbelievable events that make the traditional story of the Trojan War and the Dorian invasion at least plausible as explanations of the end of the Bronze Age world.

CHAPTER SIX

SANTORINI AND THE
LEGEND OF ATLANTIS

We have had to face a painful truth. Our university bookstore
sells more copies of books on Atlantis than books on archaeology written by professional archaeologists. The Atlantis books are
written by a variety of amateurs, including journalists, hobbyists, and
not a few people with what appears to be a tenuous grasp on reality.
For years we have wondered why there are so many books on Atlantis.
Who is reading them? What is the secret of their success? And is there
an archaeological basis for the Atlantis legend?

The facts related to the legend of Atlantis are not complicated. The
original story was told in two dialogues by the Athenian philosopher
Plato, writing about 2,400 years ago. Even Plato's near contemporaries
were divided over the question of whether the Atlantis story was true
or only a fictional tale told by Plato for philosophical purposes. The
generations that have followed have made little progress in answer-
ing that question. Plato claims that the story of Atlantis was handed
down to him from one of his ancestors, Solon, who in turn got it from
Egyptian priests.

In Plato's version of Solon's account, Atlantis was a continent in the
Atlantic Ocean with an advanced urban civilization. Its arrogant inhabitants invaded the Mediterranean about 9,000 years before Plato's
time (that is, 11,000 B.P.), were defeated in a pitched battle by the
Athenians, and were eventually destroyed, along with their entire continent, in some kind of catastrophe that swallowed them up "in a day
and a night."

Many universally acknowledged facts make it difficult to accept this story at face value: the chronology is hopelessly wrong because it places the developed civilizations of Atlantis, Athens, and Egypt in the Mesolithic period (when there were no civilizations anywhere); the geography is physically impossible, as we have known since the 1960s, when the discovery of plate tectonics dealt a death blow to the existence of a sunken continent in the Atlantic; there is not a single artifact from the ancient world that bears the name Atlantis; and finally there is not a single mention of Atlantis in any ancient text apart from Plato's (even Egyptian records, which Plato claims were Solon's original source, are silent on Atlantis).

These problems have done nothing to dampen the enthusiasm of amateurs and romantics who seem capable of finding Atlantis almost anywhere. In the seventeenth century, European scholars thought that the newly discovered American continents were Plato's Atlantis, and enthusiasts in later centuries have claimed Sweden, England, the Sahara Desert, the Azores, the Canary Islands, the North Pole, Antarctica, Bolivia, the Bahamas, Utah, Pennsylvania, and Alabama (among hundreds of other places) as the "true" Atlantis. Despite such attempts to locate Atlantis, speculation on the subject had nearly died out until the publication in 1882 of Ignatius Donnelly's book *Atlantis: The Antediluvian World*, which almost singlehandedly gave rise to the modern cottage industry of Atlantis speculation.

Donnelly, a Minnesota lawyer and politician, began with a literal reading of Plato's Atlantis and assumed that the ancient continent had once existed somewhere in the Atlantic Ocean. Donnelly argued that similarities of ancient cultures on either side of the Atlantic could be explained by postulating that a centrally located "mother" culture had peopled this Atlantic continent. He said that common features of artifacts and the use of pyramids and stone arches in building construction linked distant cultures to the Atlantis motherland. Although he relied on general features of common artifacts, which can be explained by their similar functions in ancient societies, he made a convincing case. The cultures he used as examples, the Maya and Egypt, are not only dissimilar when studied in detail, but they are separated by vast distances and a chronological gulf of 3,000 years or more and thus cannot be connected to a hypothetical motherland. Archaeologists have more plausibly explained similarities such as pyramids by the structural principles used in early engineering: a structure that narrows as it goes up is the most stable form.

Likewise, similar artifacts could be explained by invoking what is called the "limitation of possibilities." Early cultures worked with stone, basketry, pottery, wood, and textiles to manufacture their tools, weapons, clothing, storage containers, and other artifacts, and there are only a very few ways to carve, weave, sculpt, and mold such materials. In other words, the similar structural properties of widely available raw materials ensured that artifacts from widely separated cultures would share common features. Anyone looking at the painted pottery from the Anasazi culture of the American Southwest dated around A.D. 1200 and Neolithic pottery from the eastern Mediterranean world ca. 8000 B.C. will notice strong similarities in form, decoration, color, and use. There is no possibility that these unrelated cultures came into contact with each other, and the similarities are easily explained: almost everywhere that simple pottery is made by hand, the limitations of handling clay without a potter's wheel, the availability of colored minerals, and the low temperatures of the open fire will ensure that similar results are obtained. There is simply no reason to invoke alien astronauts or lost continents to explain such basic things.

But the literalists who followed Donnelly have continued the search for Atlantis, and as a result, Donnelly's book remains in print. Even Donnelly, one suspects, would doubt his rather simple original hypothesis after reviewing the century of archaeological, geological, and other scientific data accumulated since he developed it. For example, Donnelly used the original oceanographic data obtained from the ship *Challenger* to argue that the mountains discovered beneath the Atlantic Ocean were the remains of a sunken continent. He had no way of knowing that the long mountain range beneath the ocean was part of a long ridge created by the upwelling magma from the earth's mantle. These mountains are not continental at all, but among the youngest rocks on the earth, making the existence of a sunken continent simply impossible.

Donnelly, perhaps, would be forced to change his views, but no amount of mere evidence seems to shake the faith of the literalists of our own time who buy the book and pore over it as an original source. Instead of fading away, the tide of Atlantis books (almost all of them modeled in some way on Donnelly's work) has not yet reached its peak. We have been told that there are some 3,000 books on the subject of Atlantis, with more on the way. If there are no archaeological facts to work with, if there is no real Atlantis to find, then why are people still looking for it? What is the appeal of the Atlantis legend?

After many years of regarding the spectacle from afar, we have reached two conclusions. First, speculation can run rampant precisely *because* there are no firm archaeological facts pointing to the existence of Atlantis. Paradoxically, in the absence of decisive positive evidence for Atlantis, every theory explaining its whereabouts is equally correct (or, of course, equally false). This is the argument from negative evidence, or the argument *ex silentio*. Second, the desire for a lost continent and a lost civilization are part of the age-old longing, in the West at least, for a Golden Age in which things were better, simpler, and purer (forgetting of course the warlike tendencies of Plato's Atlantis). This longing is part of the usual human hunger for the marvelous and wonderful, and Atlantis literalists are ever optimistic that the definitive evidence they seek will be found in the next spadeful of earth from an excavation.

It would be tempting to dismiss the Atlantis speculation altogether and simply move on to another subject, but to do that would require us to ignore Plato's original Atlantis account. After all, Plato explicitly states that it is a *true* story that he is telling, not a legend, and this claim of truth has inspired a small group of serious scholars to attempt to reconcile the legend of Atlantis as related by Plato with archaeologically verified events. If the fantasists described earlier can be described as "literalists," then these last scholars can be called the "Euhemerist" party, because they hold that there must be *some* historical nugget, or kernel of truth, at the heart of this otherwise fantastic story. Euhemerus was a Greek philosopher and student of myths in the fourth century B.C. who held that myths are only traditional accounts of real historical persons and events. Euhemerist scholars tend to be embarrassed by the wilder effusions of the literalists and other popular writers, journalists, cranks, and quacks, but to their credit, they have persevered.

The case of the Euhemerist scholars, namely that there was a real Atlantis in some form, has steadily gained acceptance and credibility ever since the publication of Donnelly's book and the discovery of the previously unknown prehistoric Minoan culture on Crete in 1900 by Sir Arthur Evans. As early as 1939, the Greek archaeologist Spyridon Marinatos remarked on a resemblance between the Minoan culture and Plato's account of Atlantis, and what is more, he postulated that an eruption of the volcanic island of Santorini (ancient Thera) in the southern Cyclades may have been the physical cause of the demise of the Minoans (see Figure 6.1). The dramatic disappearance of the

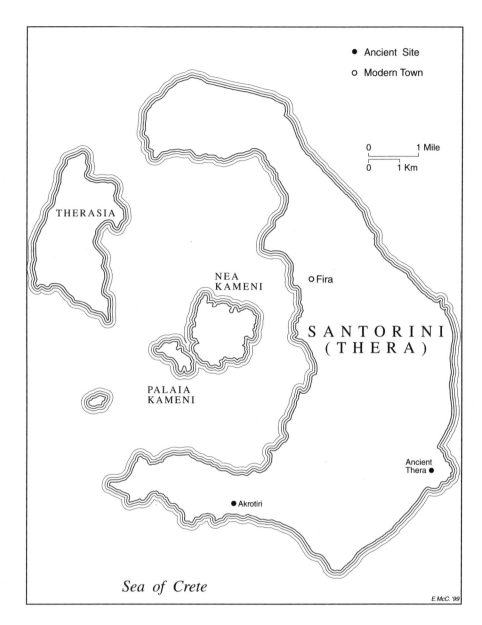

Ancient Site

Modern Town

0   1 Mile

0   1 Km

THERASIA

NEA
KAMENI

○ Fira

SANTORINI
(THERA)

PALAIA
KAMENI

Ancient
Thera ●

● Akrotiri

Sea of Crete

E.McC. '99

6.1 The island of Santorini, location of the Late Bronze Age site of Akrotiri. Fira is the modern capital of the island, and ancient Thera was the main settlement in classical times. Before the great Minoan eruption of 1628 B.C. the island was much larger: the huge central caldera was a volcanic cone that collapsed after the eruption to form the deep bay. Today new volcanic cones (Palaia Kameni and Nea Kameni) are rising from the depths to repeat the process. Akrotiri is the best known, and the only excavated Late Bronze Age site, but artifacts and traces of architectural foundations are known from Therasia and as many as twenty other locations on the island, which when excavated will enrich our understanding of the island's culture.

flourishing island culture of Minoan Crete in a volcanic eruption could be the kernel of truth, reasoned Marinatos, that underpins the Atlantis legend.

THE MINOAN ERUPTION OF SANTORINI

The intervention of World War II and the Greek Civil War prevented Marinatos from taking the field, and it was not until 1968 that he had the opportunity to begin excavations on Santorini at the site of Akrotiri. Within the first weeks of excavation, he had discovered a large town at Akrotiri that had been buried by pumice after a catastrophic eruption. The Akrotiri culture of Santorini (ancient Thera) turned out to have many similarities with the Minoan culture of Crete, which suggested to Marinatos that they had once been a single culture. The violent end of the Akrotiri town as the result of a volcanic eruption seemed likely to be responsible also for the decline of the Minoans. These findings created considerable excitement, even among usually phlegmatic archaeologists, and in the 1970s Marinatos's important discoveries were embraced by many who wished to see the Minoan eruption of the Santorini volcano as the kernel of truth in the Atlantis legend.

We were students at the time of the first excavations and well remember this excitement. It seemed as if the Minoan eruption could be called upon to settle many vexing historical and archaeological questions. Popular writers, historians, and classicists alike invoked the eruption to explain everything from the Exodus of the Hebrews to the details of classical Greek myth, while archaeologists attributed the decline or collapse of Late Bronze Age civilizations around the Mediterranean to this one eruption. For a few heady seasons it seemed that all of our historical conundra would be polished off in a single stroke, like Alexander cutting the Gordian knot. Alas, most of the more dramatic

6.2   A spouted jug from Akrotiri with eyes, a necklace, and painted breasts.

6.3   A young woman from a
wall painting in a house at Akrotiri.

hypotheses of volcanically induced cultural collapse were themselves
to collapse under the weight of accumulating evidence to the contrary.

The problem was the date of the Minoan eruption of Santorini.
Marinatos had initially dated the eruption to ca. 1450 B.C., assuming
that Akrotiri and the Minoan palaces had been destroyed at the same
time (the date of 1450 B.C. for the first wave of destructions on Crete
was long established). Careful study of the pottery and other artifacts
from Akrotiri and the comparison of these with similar materials from
the Minoan palaces ultimately convinced Marinatos that the eruption
had taken place a generation or two before the final destruction of
Minoan Crete, about 1500 B.C. While this was not exactly the simultaneous destruction that he had originally envisaged, it was close
enough to sustain the link between cause and effect. This redating was
strongly supported by the discovery of ash and pumice from the eruption *under* the floors of several of the Minoan palaces, which demonstrated clearly that the palaces had survived and flourished *after* the
eruption. The date of 1500 B.C. was widely accepted by 1974. If ac-
curate, the Minoan eruption of Santorini could not have caused any
of the late Bronze Age catastrophes such as the collapse of the Hittite
Empire. But even more surprises were yet to come.

In the 1980s carbon-14 dating of plant remains from Akrotiri gave
consistently earlier dates for the Minoan eruption, much closer to
1600 B.C. These early dates also seemed to be supported by findings
far from the Aegean. Narrow growth rings in trees around the world,

spikes of acid in Greenland ice caps, and anomalous growth of trees in the eastern provinces of Turkey have been interpreted by scientists as the result of a massive volcanic eruption that occurred in the spring of 1628 B.C., and similar global atmospheric effects do not exist at 1500 B.C. or for that matter at 1450 B.C. Although these results may themselves be overturned by future research (a separate volcanic eruption could be responsible for the 1628 B.C. date), most archaeologists have concluded that the Minoan eruption did not occur at the end of the Late Bronze Age but at its *beginning*. Thus the eruption did not cause the demise of Minoan Crete, not even combined with tidal waves or ash fall. The eruption occurred a full two centuries before the first wave of destructions reduced the Minoan palaces to ruins, and a whopping 400 years before the end of the Bronze Age.

So how does this affect the Atlantis hypothesis? In short, it helps. The island culture represented on Santorini by Akrotiri was proba-

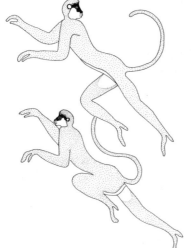

6.4 Monkeys (macaques) from a wall painting at Akrotiri. The monkeys were brought from Africa as pets.

6.5 Wall painting from Akrotiri showing lilies growing in fantastic volcanic rocks and swallows in the air above.

bly more influential in shaping Minoan and Mycenaean culture in its early stages than has generally been thought. Marinatos had considered Akrotiri an offshoot or perhaps a colony of the Minoans, but the early date of the destruction may mean that the reverse was true. Recent chance finds and deliberate prospection on Santorini, which is difficult to do because of the thick covering of pumice and ash from the eruption, indicate that there may be as many as 20 settlements of different sizes on the island. The rich finds from Akrotiri and its remarkable frescoes and outstanding architecture may point to a rich and progressive society that exported its culture to the islands and the mainland. The Akrotiri frescoes depict flotillas of ships passing between islands and landing on larger landmasses. Some of the scenes appear to be peaceful, but in others there are images of heavily armed troops, and in some fresco fragments dead men are depicted floating in the sea. Are the troops from Akrotiri or some other Santorini site? Were the dead men killed in battle? Or are the images from myth or legend?

These fresco scenes recall the Platonic story of the Atlantean invasion of the Mediterranean and their defeat by the Athenians (of Mycenaean Athens?). The peaceful appearance of Akrotiri's culture may be deceiving. If Santorini occupied a central position in the Aegean world, as is possible, and if its residents' influence on their neighbors was not always peaceable, then their sudden extinction by earthquake or volcanic eruption could very well have generated the type of story that came to Plato's ears as the legend of Atlantis.

This is the principal conclusion reached by the Euhemerists, but Santorini is not the only candidate for Atlantis. Our colleague and friend Eberhard Zangger, a Swiss geoarchaeologist, has argued that the Atlantis story was based on none other than Troy, the city in northwestern Turkey that is at the center of the Homeric legend of the Trojan War. His sophisticated and very interesting theory is supported with a close rereading of Plato and an analysis of the archaeological evidence from Troy. His argument rests on two pillars: the first is that the story of the Trojan War was altered in transmission over the

6.6 A stone stairway at Akrotiri broken by an earthquake that accompanied the Minoan eruption of Santorini's volcano. This smashed stairway symbolizes the destructive power of the eruption that completely destroyed the civilization of Santorini.

generations by Egyptian priests; thus when they told it to Plato's ancestor Solon as the story of Atlantis he did not recognize the true origins of the tale. The other pillar is the archaeology of Troy, which, Zangger argues, fits closely the Platonic description of the main metropolis of Atlantis. According to Zangger's theory, the small citadel of Bronze Age Troy became part of a much larger city that dominated a plain engineered with great hydraulic works such as artificial harbors and canals. And indeed, the work of a German team at Troy in the 1990s has brought to light evidence that seems to confirm Zangger's claim that Troy was once a central player in the cultural world of the eastern Mediterranean during the Late Bronze Age.

As attractive as this theory is, however, it has not convinced all of the Euhemerists or pushed Santorini from the spotlight. Indeed, competing theories have been inspired by Zangger's bold attempt to unravel this problem, and those of us on the sidelines will always have trouble deciding which of them is likely to be true for one simple reason. Without exception, each theory requires some of the central elements of Plato's story to be discarded.

Euhemerists have universally abandoned the date of 11,000 B.P. and the Atlantic as the site of Atlantis. But is this justified? Once we begin to *selectively* discard those parts of the story that are obviously wrong, or distorted, or fictional, and retain *only* those parts that seem to be historically valid, we are on a slippery slope toward a chaos of individual opinions and nothing more. Do we instead discard the whole legend as inherently unprovable and choose to believe that Plato simply made it up? For our part, we prefer to keep an open mind, continue to ask skeptical questions, and hope that someday new and compelling evidence will come to light, such as an inscribed tablet from Akrotiri with the word "Atlantis" on it.

CHAPTER SEVEN

A TOUR OF THE
PRINCIPAL MONUMENTS
OF PREHISTORIC GREECE

The most important sites and exhibits relating to the Palaeolithic and Neolithic are not usually included in the average tourist's itinerary. Classical sites are more numerous, better known, and more easily visited. They have been developed for tourism and are equipped with guides, placards, walkways, and sometimes guidebooks, whereas Stone Age sites are rarely visited and have few amenities. Fortunately, a few key sites are accessible to tourists, and local museums provide good displays of their artifacts.

A not-very-demanding Stone Age itinerary might include short stays in the following towns: Ioannina (Epirus), Volos (Thessaly), Nafplion (Argolid), Athens, and Iraklion (Crete) (see Figure 7.1). Many sites are only a short day trip from these bases. For those with sufficient time, a visit to Petralona Cave in the Chalkidiki could be combined with a stay in Thessaloniki.

THE PALAEOLITHIC

The best place to see Palaeolithic remains is Epirus. The Ioannina Archaeological Museum has an extensive display of Palaeolithic stone tools, animal bones, and other finds. The materials on display come

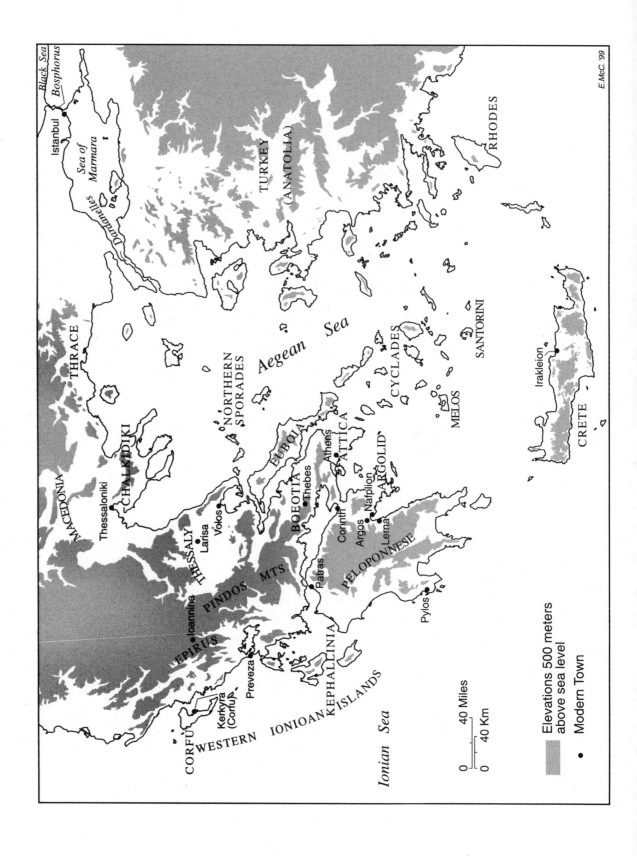

E.McC. '99

Black Sea

Bosphorus

Istanbul

Sea of
Marmara

Dardanelles

TURKEY
(ANATOLIA)

RHODES

THRACE

Aegean Sea

SANTORINI

MACEDONIA

CHALKIDIKI

NORTHERN
SPORADES

CYCLADES

MELOS

Thessaloniki

Irakleion

Larisa

THESSALY

Vólos

EUBOIA

CRETE

PINDOS MTS.

BOEOTIA

Thebes

Athens

ATTICA

Ioannina

Corinth

Nafplion

ARGOLID

EPIRUS

Patras

Argos

Lerna

PELOPONNESE

Preveza

Kerkyra
(Corfu)

CORFU

KEPHALLINIA

Pylos

WESTERN IONIOAN ISLANDS

Ionian Sea

Elevations 500 meters
above sea level

•   Modern Town

40 Miles

40 Km

0

0

from the British excavations in the 1960s at Asprochaliko Cave and Kastritsa Cave. The displays also include finds from open-air sites in Epirus, including the hand-axe we discovered in 1991, which dates to ca. 250,000 years ago.

The Palaeolithic exhibits are not as colorful as the exhibits of the classical Greek period, but they are both intriguing and evocative. Particularly noteworthy are the many small stone tools. Their cutting edges have been carefully shaped by retouching (chipping of the edges), and very few of them have definite or easily recognized shapes. Our drawings in Chapter 2 will help you recognize scrapers (edged tools used to scrape hides) and spearpoints, which prehistoric humans may have shaped while sitting around the fire. The animal bones on display were recovered from cave excavations; hence their good state of preservation. They include the bones of unfamiliar animals such as bison, aurochs (wild ox), elk, antelope, and rhinoceros. There is no more vivid evidence of how the landscape and climate have changed since the Pleistocene than the remains of now-vanished animals.

Present-day Ioannina sits on what was once an open plain on the margin of the lake that is visible from a garden terrace near the museum. Great beasts roamed the land where now the traffic rattles through the streets. The quiet world of Palaeolithic humans, where people were rare and animals were abundant, is, of course, gone forever, but the scattered relics in the display cases allow the visitor to visualize this ancient world.

The excavated cave sites of Asprochaliko and Kastritsa can be visited most easily by car. Kastritsa is located on the southern margin of the Lake Pamvotis about 30 minutes from Ioannina by car. Asprochaliko is on the main highway from Ioannina south to Preveza, near the dam on the Louros River and requires about an hour to reach. They are very small rock shelters rather than proper caverns and are fenced to protect them. It is not usually possible to arrange to have them opened (though determined souls should address inquiries to the Ioannina Archaeological Museum, where there is an office of the Antiquities Service responsible for the sites). They can be viewed profitably from outside the fence, and in any case their splendid natural setting is the most striking thing about them. The locations of both sites are marked by small signs and directions are given in the *Blue Guide* by Robin Barber.

7.1 *Opposite.* Locations of modern towns mentioned in the text.

An indispensable companion on this trip is Hammond Innes's novel, *Lefkas Man*. It is the only novel we know of that is based on Palaeolithic archaeology in Greece. Innes visited Epirus when Asprochaliko Cave was being excavated by Eric Higgs, and his story includes good descriptions of the countryside as well as a large cast of colorful characters, especially the archaeologists, who are all a bit eccentric. It makes fun reading for anyone who is in the area, and paperback editions can easily be found in used bookstores and on the Internet.

There are no Palaeolithic sites developed for visitation in Thessaly, but the archaeological museums in Larisa and particularly in Volos (see Figure 7.2) have small and attractive displays of stone tools and fossilized animal bones (including some large elephant tusks) that were found in the region. The principal sites on the banks of the Peneios River cannot be easily located, but a visit to the river in connection with the Neolithic tour suggested below will give one a good sense of place.

The Petralona cavern near the northern city of Thessaloniki is a spectacular natural phenomenon well worth a visit in its own right. It has been developed by the National Tourist Organization and regular tours are available. The famous Petralona skull, which was found here, is not on display, and the private museum on site has in any case been closed for some time. If it reopens, the exhibits should be viewed with some skepticism because the artifacts (but not the fossil animal bones) were not all found in the cave, and some nonartifactual materials are displayed alongside genuine ones.

7.2 The facade of the Volos Archaeological Museum. Many older museums are built in a pleasing neoclassical style.

A visit to Nafplion should include a stop at Franchthi Cave. The cave is the most important archaeological site in Greece for the study of the Stone Age because of its long sequence of habitation layers. It is also an exciting natural feature with a fine setting on the Aegean Sea. Although the site was excavated long ago (1967–1979), it has not been developed for tourism. The difficulty in reaching it, however, can add to one's adventure. The cave is approached from either Koilas (Koilada) or Fournoi, both villages about 80 kilometers from Nafplion. The cave is accessible by private fishing boat (hired in the village of Koilada). Alternatively, from Fournoi, a footpath directly to the cave starts from a parking lot by the chapel of Ayios Ioannis on the beach near the village. The road to Ayios Ioannis is clearly marked; one turns off the main road from Nafplion just after Fournoi. From the chapel of Ayios Ioannis the well-marked path to Franchthi Cave runs southward along the beach and over the headland to the cave in about twenty minutes. The map in the *Blue Guide* and local inquiry are indispensable for planning this leg of the tour.

Franchthi Cave has two parts, the inner chamber of the cavern and the small Neolithic settlement directly on the shore in front of the mouth of the cave. The shore settlement is the remnant of a village occupied from nearly 7000 B.C. to the beginning of the Bronze Age. Most of the village has vanished under the rising sea, but traces of it have been found in hand-drilled cores taken by divers nearly 100 meters off shore. In the open trenches on the beach are the remains of retaining walls and house walls. Many burials and large quantities of painted pottery were found here, and a selection of the finer specimens is on exhibit in the Nafplion Archaeological Museum.

Excavation trenches inside the cave penetrate the depths of the stratified deposits, through Neolithic, Mesolithic, and Palaeolithic levels in turn. The deepest trenches are very interesting, if quite dangerous (stay well away from the crumbling edges), because they show the great thickness of these deposits (up to twelve meters). Each small layer visible in the sides of the trenches took many generations to accumulate, and human occupation has been verified all the way down. One gets a sense of the long occupation of the cave that is very affecting. Palaeolithic layers are the dark red stony layers at the bottom; the fine-grained, ashy gray Mesolithic layers are above them (up to three meters thick). The Neolithic is found near the top third of the visible sections. The present surface inside the cave has many potsherds and flints but is essentially modern. The artifacts were brought to the surface in medieval and early historical times by diggers look-ing for organic matter to make fertilizer and gunpowder.

The cave is a cool spot in summer to sit and meditate on this mar-vel of time. The sound of gulls, and the keening of the falcons that live in the cave, are reminders that the throngs of former inhabitants who lived there also heard these sounds and looked out on the Bay of Koilada. (The sea was almost always up to seven kilometers out from its present position, so the view was usually of a shallow river valley.)

When we were digging at the site in the early 1970s, we excavated a horse's teeth from the deep central trench and remember thinking that the sun had once fallen on the now-submerged valley outside the cave and that this very horse had grazed on long-gone meadows until Palaeolithic hunters killed it and dragged it back to the cave to be butchered for food. We imagined the fires in the cave (we had found an ashy hearth in this layer) and fingered the sharp splinters of flint that tipped the hunters' projectiles.

THE NEOLITHIC

Neolithic sites are somewhat more numerous than those of the Palae-olithic, and visits to these are very rewarding. In addition to the Neo-lithic remains at Franchthi (some pottery is on exhibit in the Nafplion Archaeological Museum), in the area of Nafplion, a good Neolithic house foundation can be viewed at Lerna (near the town of Myloi, outside of Argos), and the Argos Archaeological Museum has a very good exhibit of Neolithic artifacts from the site. There is also some Neolithic material in the Iraklion Archaeological Museum of Crete. In Athens the National Archaeological Museum has one of the largest exhibits of Neolithic artifacts, which includes objects from all parts of Greece. A trip to the Goulandris Cycladic Museum on Kolonaki Square is also recommended. Although its exhibits are primarily ori-ented to the later Bronze Age cultures of the Cyclades, Neolithic arti-facts are also on display.

The best way to get a good look at Neolithic life and culture, how-ever, is to tour Thessaly and visit the sites of Sesklo and Dimini and the archaeological museums in Volos and Larisa. For the Thessalian trip, one of the cool and pretty villages on Mount Pelion, perhaps Makrynitsa or Portaria, is a good base. The Volos Archaeological Mu-seum has the most modern and richest exhibits on Neolithic life. The prehistoric hall displays graves, house models, agricultural tools, food remains, and a dazzling array of well-preserved pots, figurines, and other artifacts (see Figure 7.3). The photographs and a reconstructed stratigraphic section there provide good preparation for visiting the sites. The museum's attractive displays highlight house construction, craftwork, farming, technology, and the arts. There is a distinct regional style evident in all the artifacts, particularly the painted pottery, which contrasts markedly with the styles of the Peloponnesian materials on display in Nafplion and Argos.

The Thessalian pottery is light colored with vivid, dark red, painted geometric designs. In later periods, the decoration is brown, but at all times abstract designs predominate, though in a tremendous variety of shapes and design combinations. The figurines of human forms are also eye-catching artifacts, with elaborate hairstyles and strange "fishy" faces with cowrie-shell eyes.

The archaeological museum in Larisa is worth visiting to see the small display of Neolithic pottery, figurines, and a spectacular stela (stone slab) with a carved figure of a warrior. This visit can take in the archaeological sites of Sesklo (eighteen kilometers from Volos) and Dimini (six kilometers from Volos) along the way, and is an excellent introduction to the Neolithic world. Both sites were excavated for the first time in the first decade of the twentieth century by the Greek archaeologist Christos Tsountas, a true pioneer. Since then, they have been reexcavated by teams of Greek archaeologists and prepared for visits by tourists. The sites have good walkways and explanatory placards, and the buildings have been cleaned and conserved, allowing the visitor to get a good idea of the layout of the sites.

The excavators left an impressive thick column of sediments in the middle of Sesklo that shows the thickness of the original deposits. This stratigraphic martyr, as archaeologists call it, has layers with burned adobe bricks, potsherds, and even carbonized (burned) plant remains. On our last visit, we were intrigued to see clearly identifiable acorns, lentils, and cereals in this martyr, a fascinating glimpse of the food eaten at the site more than 7,000 years ago.

The site of Sesklo provides a good picture of a Neolithic village.

7.3 A stone seal from Neolithic Sesklo. Dipped in pigment or pressed into clay, the design on the seal could indicate private ownership.

Over a fence near the parking lot is a small area with house foundations excavated by Demetrios Theocharis, a Greek archaeologist from Larisa, in the 1970s. These houses seem to have been built according to a plan: they line a road and have open spaces between them. Theocharis believed that the entire area from there to the upper acropolis of the site was filled with habitations and that Sesklo was a town of perhaps 5,000 people, rather than a village. Other archaeologists working at the site have reduced the population estimate to between 1,000 and 2,000, but either way, Sesklo was a settlement of impressive size in its day.

The main part of the site is a small magoula (tell), deeply eroded on the eastern and northern edges by a ravine. The top of the tell is dominated by a large building called a megaron (the ancient Greek word for a hall or mansion). This large structure was established on a solid stone foundation in the heart of the site as early as 5,000 B.C. It appears to be protected by a defensive wall of stone that curves around the front of the structure. Radiating out from the central building is a jumble of foundations for rooms both large and small, but all rectangular in plan and substantial in size. The houses once had mud-brick walls, some of which are visible in a preserved profile, a section through the mound left by the archaeologists to allow them to view the stratification of the site. Some layers of the tell visible in this profile contain burned brick and charcoal (marking house fires) and much clay thick with potsherds and other debris. This material is all decayed mud brick turned back to clay by the rain and used by the Neolithic villagers to fill old foundations, raising the surface of the mound gradually over the centuries. It is to the use of mud-brick architecture that we owe the good preservation of Neolithic artifacts in Thessaly. Some Neolithic tells are 50 feet thick, testifying to the long-term survival and success of Neolithic civilization.

In Dimini is another very late Neolithic megaron on the summit of a small hill (partly natural, partly artificial), which is surrounded by rings of walls and house foundations. At Dimini, however, the much thinner deposits on the hill were eroded in antiquity, making this site difficult to interpret. There is a Mycenaean tholos (round) tomb at the site well worth a visit, but it belongs to a much later period (ca. 1350 – 1250 B.C.). Most of what is visible at Dimini is dated 5000 – 4000 B.C.

The compact nature of the typical Neolithic village is readily apparent here. The low walls in roughly concentric lines around the megaron may have been defensive, or they may have served to organize the site and control access to the megaron. The foundations on the slopes between the walls all belong to small private houses. Today Dimini is located well inland, but work by the geoarchaeologist Eberhard Zangger has shown that this site was once quite close to the Bay of Volos before alluvium washed down by a nearby river over the past 5,000 years pushed the coast farther out. Perhaps Dimini required defensive walls to protect it from pirates when it was closer to the sea?

The impressive Mycenaean tholos tomb at Dimini is one of the few known tholos tombs in northern Greece and may have belonged to a settlement connected with Homeric Iolkos, the famous coastal home of Jason the Argonaut. The Mycenaean settlement attached to this tholos must lie somewhere beneath the young river alluvium covering the plain. The exact site of Iolkos itself is disputed, but it is likely to be close to present-day Volos, left high and dry by the same alluvium that washed past Dimini.

The large and impressively built Neolithic megara at Sesklo and Dimini have sometimes been interpreted as temples because of their generic similarity in layout to ancient Greek and Roman temples. The central placement of the megaron at the summit of the Neolithic tell and at the center of the village may be additional evidence of their special significance. The everyday artifacts found at Sesklo and Dimini include fireplaces, cooking and storage pots, and agricultural implements of stone such as querns for grinding grain, flint sickles, and obsidian knives. These quotidian items are typical of a simple domestic household rather than a temple, and most archaeologists today regard these megara as the residences of high-status persons ("chiefs" or "big men") in the community who enjoyed the privilege of residing in the largest and best-built house. Many other smaller and decidedly domestic structures on Neolithic sites, however, also have simple megaron layouts.

After a visit to Sesklo and Dimini, we recommend a drive to the neighboring town of Larisa to see a few tells, view the Peneios River, and visit the archaeological museum located in an old Ottoman mosque in the city center. A much larger museum for Larisa is in the works, but for now the old museum contains more good Neolithic figurines (collected by enthusiastic and patriotic amateurs) as well as many Palaeolithic tools and fossils, including the huge tusks of primitive straight-tusked elephants. Of particular note is the large carved stone slab (stela) found on the Souphli Magoula north of town. It is a prehistoric monument (ca. 3500 B.C.) and evidently depicts a warrior.

It perhaps marked the grave of a hero in the late Neolithic period when warfare was apparently on the rise.

Another pleasant and easily visited Neolithic site is Lerna, near Argos in the Peloponnese. This important site is used as a guide by archaeologists for the interpretation of the Neolithic and Bronze Age periods in the Argolid and beyond. Neolithic and Bronze Age artifacts from the excavations are on display in the Argos Archaeological Museum. Both the site and the museum are about twelve kilometers from Nafplion (the best place to stay).

Lerna is a low tell typical of the Neolithic village sites in southern Greece. About one-third of this site was excavated by John Caskey of the University of Cincinnati in the 1950s, and it is best known for its extensive Early Bronze Age remains. Little of the Neolithic settlement could be tested by excavation because of the need to protect and preserve the overlying Bronze Age remains, but one good Neolithic house was uncovered in a deep trench used to probe the underlying layers at the site. The house is clearly visible at the bottom of this trench near the entrance of the site. One can see the foundations of the Neolithic house with its simplified megaron plan. This small house at the Neolithic level is separated from the well-preserved Early Helladic (that is, Early Bronze Age) House of the Tiles above it by accumulated occupation debris that reaches a depth of two meters or more. That is how much the tell grew in height from 5500 to 2500 B.C.

The objects of greatest interest from Lerna are exhibited in a special room in the Argos museum. Some typical figurines, including a fine female figurine with painted decoration, are among the best ever found. Stone axes, painted pots, and flint tools round out the display. Most noteworthy is how the pottery here and at Franchthi and the other Peloponnesian sites differs from that found in Thessaly. These use dark reddish brown designs on a lighter brown background. The dominant motifs are also abstract geometric elements, but the choice of colors and the forms of the pots reveal a distinct regional style. In the Nafplion Archaeological Museum the few Franchthi pots on display are markedly similar in style to the Lerna pots. Similarities carry over into the architecture (visible at Franchthi Cave as scrappy but recognizable stone walls and terraces in the trenches by the sea). Several archaeologists, particularly K. D. Vitelli and Tracey Cullen, two American archaeologists, have agreed that similarities among the Lerna and Franchthi pots (as well as those from Corinth, Nemea, and a few other sites) are strong enough to prove that there was some local trade in pots; and potters, too, may have moved from one settlement to another. These were probably young women who moved to their husbands' villages when they married, taking their potting skills with them. This prospect, worked out after detailed analysis of the pots, gives us a fascinating peep into the social and economic life of the Neolithic villagers.

THE BRONZE AGE

The opportunities for visiting Bronze Age sites are numerous and growing. For a tour, the sites can be grouped into three geographic areas: Crete, the Cycladic islands, and mainland Greece.

On Crete, Sir Arthur Evans ushered in the Age of the Tourist with his skillful, imaginative, and extremely controversial reconstructions of the greatest of the Minoan palaces, the Palace of Minos at Knossos. Italian, French, American, and Greek archaeologists have not been as interested as Evans in reconstructions, but all have followed suit in preparing their sites for visitors. With the exception of the most recently discovered palaces (for instance at Chania in western Crete, which lies beneath the modern city), the Cretan palaces have been extensively cleared to reveal their plans. With many useful and locally available guidebooks to the palaces, one may visit Knossos, Mallia, Phaistos, Ayia Triada, Gournia, and Zakro in a week, and get a good idea of how the palaces were arranged and functioned.

A more extended itinerary should take in villas such as Myrtos (on the south coast) and Amnisos (on the north coast) and the astonishingly complex and interesting burial complex at Arkhanes, on the road from Knossos south toward Phaistos. Here are the early tholos tombs, chamber tombs, and shrines that help complete the picture of Minoan life. The village of Gournia is a must, and a walk in the well-preserved streets, peeking into the houses of everyday people, is a pleasant way to visualize everyday life in the Bronze Age.

It is possible to visit some Early Minoan sites as well. Examples of the communal early Minoan tholos tombs can be seen at Ayia Triada, near the palace. The most important village site is Vasiliki, on the road

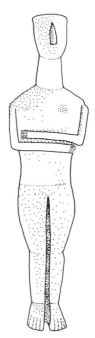

7.4   A marble Early Cycladic figurine or idol.

through to Ierapetra, and the spectacular setting is worth the stop. Energetic travelers should take the boat trip to the Early Minoan island community of Mochlos because of its many tombs built in the clefts of the rocks. These interesting tombs were constructed to resemble small versions of the Minoan houses, whose rubble foundations are also visible on the island. Finds from the Mochlos can be viewed in the archaeological museum of Ayios Nikolaos.

Generally speaking, Crete's archaeological treasures belong to the Minoan period rather than to the lesser-known classical period, and the entire island is like one large archaeological park, with well-marked and accessible sites and a growing number of regional museums with first-rate exhibits. The most important is the archaeological museum in Iraklion. The best and most important and beautiful Minoan artifacts and wall paintings are deposited here, and there is an excellent guidebook to the collections. Some smaller museums, most notably at Ayios Nikolaos, a charming harbor town east of Iraklion, have good displays of Early Minoan pottery, stone vessels, and figurines.

The Bronze Age sites on the Cycladic or other Aegean islands present new challenges and opportunities. Many of the most important Middle and Late Bronze Age sites with impressive ruins, such as Poliochni (on the island of Lemnos), Phylakopi (on Melos), Ayia Irini (on Keos, or Kea) and Thermi (on Lesvos), are only rarely visited, while the spectacular and famous site of the "Bronze Age Pompeii" at Akrotiri (on Santorini) is one of the most heavily visited sites in Greece, attracting millions of visitors annually. A visit to Akrotiri (particularly now that the new museum in Phira, the capital of the island, is open) is a must, and there are, again, excellent local guidebooks. We recommend, however, visiting one or two of the less crowded islands, where the experience is more like exploring and less like being "herded." Each of the Aegean islands has its own distinctive beauty and character.

Perhaps the easiest of the great island sites to visit is Kolonna, on Aigina, less than an hour's boat ride from Athens. Aigina has one of the least-noted but perhaps largest and most important Bronze Age sites outside Akrotiri (Santorini). Located in the main town, the Kolonna site has an impressive series of fortification walls that enclosed what may have been the biggest town in the Bronze Age Aegean. It is worth a visit.

The best Bronze Age art and artifacts, however, are on display in Athens. The National Archaeological Museum has (at this writing in early 2000) the world-famous Akrotiri wall frescoes and some of the best-known Cycladic figurines and pots of polished white marble. The National Archaeological Museum's collections have been almost eclipsed since the ultramodern Goulandris Museum of Cycladic Civilization opened near Kolonaki Square in the 1980s. The museum boasts air-conditioning, modern exhibit halls, a garden, and a nice museum shop. But it should be visited for its unparalleled collection of Cycladic sculpture in marble and its wide array of everyday artifacts from the Early Bronze Age Cyclades. For anyone with only limited time, it is not to be missed.

The Mycenaean Empire was larger, in geographic terms, than that of its neighboring rivals, the Minoans. Sites are scattered across the country from north to south and from coast to coast. Unlike on Crete, it is not possible to make a comprehensive tour in a small period of time, even with a private car. The minimal tour should include the National Archaeological Museum and the Nafplion Archaeological Museum, plus sites in Boeotia and the Argolid, with side trips to Sparta and Pylos. Although the National Archaeological Museum in Athens has the richest collection of Mycenaean artifacts, there are few Mycenaean architectural remains in Athens. A bit of Cyclopean wall can be seen

7.5 Pottery and design motifs from the Late Bronze Age site of Akrotiri on Santorini.

7.6 Decorative ornaments from a Minoan wall painting.

just inside the entrance gates of the Acropolis, and the Agora Museum has displays relating to chamber tombs from the lower town.

The best well-preserved Mycenaean architecture is in the immediate vicinity of Nafplion. The capital citadel of Mycenae itself is the place to start. Here one can visit the largest tholos tombs, peep into the tombs in Shaft Grave Circles A and B and marvel at the Lion Gate and the Cyclopean fortifications. Parts of the palace can be seen on the summit, including the heavily reconstructed throne room. The secret springs in the back citadel must also be seen (flashlight and good shoes are essential for navigating about 150 stone steps into an unlit dark tunnel). Several good guidebooks are available at the site itself and at the Nafplion Archaeological Museum. Of the most recent excavations, the House with the Idols, the source of the curious statuettes on exhibit in Nafplion, is worth a visit.

Other sites to visit in the area are Tiryns, Midea, and the small bridge at Kazarmas. The Kazarmas bridge is located very near the main road from Nafplion to the ancient theater at Epidauros and is well marked and easily accessible. A wonder not to be missed, the bridge is supported by a single corbeled arch and is built using monumental Cyclopean masonry. Not only is it an excellent example of a little-known aspect of Mycenaean architectural skill, but it is still standing and functioning as designed some 3,300 years after being built.

At Tiryns, the most important remains are the foundations of the palace. The low foundations might not be as impressive as the better-preserved fortifications, but the plan of the palace can be clearly seen: walking around the rooms and corridors is a bit like walking a garden maze, and just as much fun, if for no other reason than the many fine views of Nafplion, the Argolic Gulf, and the mountains beyond.

CHAPTER EIGHT

LAST REFLECTIONS

In these pages we have surveyed Greek prehistory in its entirety, but like any guide, we necessarily passed by important monuments, skipped dangerously over details, and finally painted a picture colored by our own memories and personal points of view. The landscape we describe has been traversed, occupied, and remade for hundreds of thousands of years by many different peoples. Is any general conclusion possible, when such different stages of culture and great sweeps of time are involved?

For us the answer to that question is yes. There is an important lesson to be drawn from the successes and failures of so many generations of humans. Most writers give in to the temptation, no doubt a legacy of the nineteenth-century Romantic movement, to see the Greek landscape and its inhabitants as a "timeless" land where the modern inhabitants follow a way of life that was established in the most distant past. Writers in this Romantic vein imagine that the natural landscape is unchanging and that the landscape and environment we see today is in its essentials the same as that seen by the classical Greeks and the Homeric heroes. Our own research has convinced us that this Romantic view is completely unjustified.

The human story here as elsewhere was not one of static structures or values set in a context of changeless physical environment. Although we have argued from the beginning that *human* nature is in some way constant, this does not mean that the relationship between human settlement and landscape has been changeless. On the contrary, the human impulse to modify their natural surroundings for their own purposes has resulted in an ever-changing cycle of modifications to the landscape that can be detected in the archaeological record. This new point of view can be referred to as coevolution, in a rather loose correspondence with biological theory.

Prehistoric societies were dynamic, in a state of constant change, even if this change has to be measured in centuries or millennia. Nearer to the present time, the pace of change accelerated continuously until change itself became the usual state of affairs. From the beginning of the Neolithic period to the end of the Bronze Age ever more complex forms of social organization took shape, sometimes succumbing to disorder and chaos for a while, only to reemerge again later. These forms of social organization are what we commonly call "civilizations."

Archaeologists do not have a surefire explanation for the pattern of rising and falling civilizations, but part of the explanation may lie in the makeup of human culture itself, which has a built-in dynamic of change based on processes of social interaction that favor and reward complexity. Perhaps we may yet recognize in this process a collective social drive akin to Nietzsche's "will to power"; or perhaps the rise and fall of civilizations is the result of social evolution driven by selective powers analogous to those seen in biological evolution. Social scientists as diverse in time and place as Thucydides, Oswald Spengler, and Arnold Toynbee have attempted to classify the internal processes that underpin "civilization" and identify once and for all the dynamic that explains cultural change. Although these attempts, which can be described as epic in scale, have undoubtedly been partially successful, scientists are still undecided as to the exact historical causes of cultural change. They cannot agree whether the changes follow a pattern, a point of view common to the three historians just mentioned, or were merely the work of random chance.

Modern historians, no doubt influenced by the dominance of Darwinian evolutionary theory in the life sciences, favor the accumulation of historically contingent events as an explanation for historical process. This is not the same thing as "randomness" in the strict sense of the term, but it nevertheless leaves no room for either the actions of individuals or the larger processes, such as Toynbee's "challenge-response" theory or Spengler's notion of the life and death of civilizations as analogous with biological processes.

Whether we agree with modern historical theory or not, we are convinced that any explanation for the rise and fall of civilization in

8.1   The Greek landscape was once predominantly rural.

prehistoric Greece must embrace the dynamic properties of the physical environment. Around the world, archaeological case studies reveal complex interactions between human settlements and their landscape, which appear to be a form of mutual and reciprocal causation akin to the coevolution of certain biological species such as bees and flowers. At this early stage of study it would be unwise to dignify the coevolution of human settlement and landscape as a full-blown theory. It is rather more of a metaphorical way of describing a complex system by identifying its components and documenting the direction and scale of the connections between them.

The physical characteristics of a landscape and the natural environment place certain limits on the possible forms of human culture. Farming is not possible in the Arctic or fishing in the desert. Human actions modify the environment over many generations by removing or displacing existing species of plants and animals and replacing them with new ones, and in many cases altering the landscape itself by clearing forests or triggering soil erosion. These changes transform the landscape, opening up new possibilities and removing others. In short, the possibilities presented by a previously unexploited landscape are continuously and progressively altered over time as each generation of humans makes social choices; these accumulated choices in turn modify the features of the physical environment, making new choices possible.

In past geologic epochs, the world climate has changed radically: forests have come and gone, glaciers have advanced and retreated, the sea has encroached upon the land and fallen away. Extinct and now-forgotten animals moved in a landscape scarcely imaginable in our present world. Human societies were molded by these landscapes and adapted to them. They were not passive elements of the landscape, however, but active agents of change. With increasing success in each succeeding period, the human presence was registered on the land. Forests retreated before polished stone, and then hardened bronze axes; later the plow turned up the soil, exposing it to erosion. Native plants and animals were supplanted by the domesticated breeds introduced from distant lands, and the features of the Greek earth were further altered by the steady application of fire, the plow, and the grazing of sheep and goats. The land we see today is thus partly the product of geologic forces of global scale over vast reaches of time and partly an artifact of human manufacture that has been 10,000 years in the making.

The Greek landscape is not unchanging, any more than the human societies that are a part of it. It is instead ever-changing—restless and

8.2 A swallow from a Late Bronze Age wall painting at Akrotiri.

dynamic. It flows like the river of time itself. If this vision of society and nature leaves no room for Romanticism with its insistence upon static, permanent forms of nature and society, it at least opens the door to a sober and realistic assessment of the human past. If our vision of dynamic change in human societies and the natural world runs contrary to our more conservative feelings, it at least leaves room for thinking once more of progress in human affairs. As archaeologists we are permitted to end on this hopeful note because our subject matter provides such a long perspective on human actions, a perspective that may elude other present-day observers.

As we write these last thoughts, the bells of a church ring out over the slopes of Mount Pelion, marking the end of another day and reminding us of the continuity of human existence in Greece and of

8.3 Terra-cotta animal figurines from various Mycenaean sites. It is thought that some of these figurines may have been used as "votives" at shrines. Their frequent appearance at sites of all types, and the fact that they represent common barnyard animals, is testimony to the importance of animal husbandry in this period.

8.4 The eighteenth-century Fetihye ("Victory") mosque in Ioannina, Epirus, one of many examples of fine Ottoman architecture in Greece.

the reality of constant change. The blows of Stone Age axes on thick chestnut trees gave way to the tinkle of bronze bells on the necks of goats in the Age of Bronze, and then to the sounds of stone masons shaping marble for temple foundations in classical antiquity, the tramp of soldiers' boots in the Roman period, the chanting of Orthodox monks in the Byzantine twilight, and the call of the Ottoman müezzin; now the sound of bells slowly gives ground to the industrial hum of a passing jet. The prehistoric past we have described in these pages was neither prologue nor prelude to later and present Greek civilizations, but instead only one part of the seamless flow of human affairs across the seemingly immeasurable sea of prehistoric time.

A Note on the Dates Used in This Work

There are many old saws about archaeologists. One that we have seen on a bumper sticker is, "Archaeologists are romantic: they will date any old thing." But corny jokes sometimes make a serious point: dates and dating techniques take up a great deal of space in archaeological textbooks for good reason. Without a chronological framework it is impossible to discuss cultural change or test hypotheses to explain past events. If one does not know which of several archaeological cultures is earlier than another, or whether several cultures existed at the same time, it is impossible to untangle the web of cause and effect.

It is widely assumed that in a given geographic area such as Greece there has been a long, slow domino effect: that is, earlier cultures affected the evolution of later ones. The selection of a good site for a settlement in the Neolithic, for instance, increased the probability that the same site would play an important role in later periods. If nothing else, the ruins visible at an earlier site advertised its advantages and disadvantages to later generations. Any attempt to work out the proper sequence of historically related events, therefore, requires a firm understanding of chronology.

Until the advent of nuclear physics in the second half of the twentieth century, the age of ancient things was determined by "relative" dating. Individual artifacts and buildings were dated within a single site by their stratigraphic position—that is, whether they were near the top or bottom of a series of layers. In an undisturbed sequence of archaeological layers, artifacts were assumed to be progressively older as one descended through the layers. Dating between sites was achieved primarily by cross-dating. That is, if artifacts found at the top of site A were identical to artifacts from the bottom of site B (as long as they were geographically close and the respective sequences of layers were undisturbed), it followed that site A was probably older, relatively speaking, than site B.

A.1 A stack of lead weights from Late Bronze Age Akrotiri on Santorini.

Another form of relative dating was achieved by cross-dating: relating Greek sites to the more established chronologies of the neighboring cultures of pharaonic Egypt and Mesopotamia, which are based on astronomical dates and king lists. Cross-dating depends on finding objects of a known date from one culture in one level of another. Thus a well-dated Egyptian artifact from a known dynasty when found in a stratum of a Minoan or Mycenaean site can be used to establish the date of that stratum, assuming that the Egyptian artifact is not an heirloom or antique (always a risky assumption). Key cross-dates were established in this way early in Aegean Bronze Age archaeology, and they still underpin the entire chronology of the period.

Precise calendar dates, or "absolute" dates, for sites and artifacts can sometimes be determined using more scientific techniques. The most widely used methods of absolute dating in archaeology today measure radioactive decay; these are called radiocarbon dating (also 14C or carbon-14 dating), thorium/uranium dating, or potassium/argon dating. Other dating techniques, such as electron spin resonance and thermoluminescence, employ related physical processes. Another absolute dating technique is dendrochronology, which involves the counting of tree rings. The technical details of these and other methods are too numerous to include here, but the interested reader can pursue them in some of the references cited in the Bibliographic Essay. The two systems of dating, the absolute and the relative methods, have been used together over the past century to build up the established chronology for the prehistoric archaeology of Greece. The dates given in this book for the Stone Age are largely based on absolute dating. Dates for the Bronze Age have largely been determined by the more traditional relative dating method.

Calendar dates are expressed in the literature in a variety of ways, and confusion can arise when different systems are used by different archaeologists. Throughout this work we have attempted to use a reasonably consistent system, but it differs from that used in other books, and the dates will not always match those in museum exhibits and guides. The discrepancies reflect the inevitable refinement of chronology as methods are improved and new samples are obtained. We have chosen to use the system of B.P. (before present) dates, which is widely used in the natural sciences to express dates in the Old Stone Age. By international convention, "present" is defined as A.D. 1950. Hence, a date of 5000 B.P. means 5,000 years before 1950. In this book, B.P. dates from before about 40,000 years ago are rough approximations only, not precise calendar dates. The B.P. dates given for Upper Palaeolithic, Mesolithic, and Neolithic sites, however, are based on dendrochronology, radiocarbon dating (itself calibrated using dendrochronology), and other means, which are expressed as true calendar dates, although there is a certain margin of error for any date.

We use a different system for the Bronze Age. Although archaeology has developed a good sequence of relative dates for the Bronze Age Aegean, by convention they are expressed as B.C. or B.C.E. (before Christ or before the common era), counting backward from 2,000 years ago. Hence, a culture that began in 4000 B.P. (4,000 years ago) is dated 2000 B.C. in this system. Because the B.C. system is used universally by writers on the Aegean Bronze Age and is found in museum guides, display captions, and in textbooks, we use it here for convenience.

There is a useful logic, however, in using the B.C. designation for Bronze Age dates. Because the Bronze Age chronology is largely a conventional one based on relative dating, and the Stone Age chronology is primarily an absolute system, the change from B.P. to B.C. largely coincides with the change in the predominant system of dating. No matter how a chronology has been built up, some statistical uncer-

A.2   Terra-cotta loom weights perforated for suspension from the warps of an upright loom.

tainty still underlies all dates, and as a consequence we sometimes add the qualifier "ca." (circa, or about) before many dates, and the reader may wish to add that mentally to all of them. These rather loose frameworks of dating may not seem sufficiently precise, but despite enormous scientific advances, events of long ago sometimes can be dated only within very broad ranges.

On the Schliemann Trail

The best-known and most controversial personality in the annals of Aegean prehistory is Heinrich Schliemann, the rags-to-riches German merchant, world traveler, and archaeologist who discovered the legendary site of Troy and excavated Shaft Grave Circle A at Mycenae with its gold treasure. Schliemann's energy, enthusiasm, and industry brought the Aegean Bronze Age to light from the obscurity of its mythical origins, and in this he was a true pioneer.

From the time of Thucydides to the middle of the nineteenth century, thoughtful people reflected on the early history of Greece as it was known from poetry, myth, and legend. In the early 1870s, Schliemann decided to search for the physical remains of the great heroes of the preclassical world by applying the methods of the brand-new science of archaeology. Nearly every Bronze Age site of importance in the Aegean was inspected or excavated in part by Heinrich Schliemann, a feat that places him in the heroic age of early archaeology as a scientific discipline.

We are thus fortunate to have the details of Schliemann's life in an excellent biography by David Traill (see Bibliographical Essay), the first scholarly biography of Schliemann to appear in any language. Traill provides many familiar details of Schliemann's life, as well as much that is new and unfamiliar. The book contains the usual accounts of Schliemann's start as a poor store clerk in Germany and his later success in business, building fortunes in Russia, the California goldfields, and Parisian real estate. Also familiar is his account of how Schliemann pursued his dream of becoming an archaeologist, settled in Athens in 1869 at the age of 47, married Sophia Engastromenos, a nineteen-year-old Greek who became his archaeological companion, and embarked on his famous excavations at Troy. But Traill also relates that Schliemann engaged in sharp business practices that verged on outright fraud, that his becoming an archaeologist was not the fulfillment of a lifelong dream (indeed he never mentioned the possibility in his

B.1   Heinrich Schliemann
at age 46.

letters or diaries until his sudden "conversion" in middle age), and that pride and megalomania led him to make extravagant claims about his finds. Schliemann fiddled with his own autobiography to make his past look more heroic and interesting than it really was, and he was not above fiddling with the truth whenever and wherever it suited him. Traill also makes it clear, though, that Schliemann had enormous gifts. Traill acknowledges Schliemann's prodigious linguistic ability (he was fluent in at least seventeen languages), his business prowess (he retired by age 46 but managed his estate personally for the rest of his life), and his enormous energy and curiosity. Until the end of his life business and archaeological research took him to Russia, the Ottoman Empire, Egypt, the United States, Cuba, and almost every country in Europe. In the last fifteen years of his life he made as many as seventeen major trips a year, repeating some journeys year after year, while at the same time successfully managing his business affairs, conducting excavations, and, almost as an afterthought it seems, spending time with his growing family in Athens. He died in Naples, alone, in December 1890 while returning from ear surgery in Germany. Characteristically, he had gone to Naples against the advice of his doctor to visit the archaeological museum and nearby Pompeii.

To all of these accomplishments we would add our own remarks about his scholarly achievements. Despite his late entry into archaeol-

ogy, his published excavation reports are detailed and exacting, revealing a respectable command of the literature, both ancient and
modern. They are good enough to stand on their own merits today.
He published four books on his Trojan excavations, two books covering his excavations at Mycenae and Tiryns, and others on his research
at Orchomenos in Boeotia and on the island of Ithaka.

Having noted the growth in theme-based travel—from walking
tours of "Dickens's London" to Mediterranean cruises with culinary
and musical themes—it occurred to us that a self-guided tour of the
"Schliemann Trail" would add zest and variety to any visit to Greece
or northwestern Turkey. Many places in the world have some association with Schliemann, but the majority of those associated with his
archaeological career are in the Aegean world, where sites and monuments connected with Schliemann's life can provide direction and
purpose to one's travels there. The best place to begin the Schliemann
Trail is in Athens, where Schliemann made his home for the last 20
years of his life.

Schliemann in Athens

The trail begins at the Iliou Melathron, the monumental two-story
house Schliemann built in the center of Athens near Constitution
Square (Plateia Syntagmatos) as his permanent residence and a home
for his family (Sophia and two children). The house was designed by
the neoclassical architect F. Ziller, who incorporated many idiosyncratic features required by Schliemann himself. One wonders what
Sophia and the children made of the life-sized statues of pagan gods
on the roof, the elaborate frescoes in the style of later Pompeiian
wall paintings that depict Greek gods, muses, and heroes, and the
quotations from Homer's *Odyssey* that grace the doors and niches in
the walls.

Throughout the house Troy is the dominant theme: Iliou Melathron means "Great House of Troy," and the decoration is based on a
pastiche of Bronze Age motifs from artifacts brought to light by
Schliemann's excavations, liberally admixed with the then-popular
scheme of neoclassical decoration based on Greco-Roman designs.
Even the iron fence in front of the house is adorned with small figures
of Athena's famous owl. Inside the house there are great halls for
Schliemann's receptions, large dining rooms, imposing corridors, and
a study where he worked while standing at a desk, simultaneously

writing and translating books, letters, and business correspondence in a dozen languages. Here too the furniture displays carvings of lions' paws and Athena's owls with outstretched wings. The scale is everywhere grand and imposing, and, one is forced to acknowledge, rather cold and drafty. The house was closed to the public for many years while it served as the seat of the Supreme Court, but it has now been fully restored and today houses the Numismatic Museum.

From the Iliou Melathron, the next station on the Schliemann Trail is the National Archaeological Museum, which displays many of the important finds made by Schliemann in his excavations at Mycenae, Tiryns, and Orchomenos. The Shaft Grave Circle at Mycenae was Schliemann's most important find in Greece. The treasures from these tombs were immediately recognized as of the first order and were quickly installed in their own exhibit hall in the center of the museum, where today one can still see the golden death masks, the ostrich egg shell vessels, the bronze weapons with precise metal inlays, and the countless objects of gold, silver, bronze, glass, rock crystal, and stone that were found in the graves. The originality and eclectic taste exhibited in these finds, which were recovered from only six graves that have been dated to a short period around 1600–1550 B.C., have excited comment and interest since the moment of their discovery in August 1876.

One can detect in these archaeological wonders the influence of central Asia, Africa, Egypt, Anatolia, and the Middle East in their manufacture and decoration. The spectacular originality and quality of this art has induced wonder in many and not a little suspicion in others. David Traill, the author of Schliemann's biography, accuses him of salting the graves with artifacts collected in his travels, and even

B.2   An octopus design from Late Bronze Age painted-pottery decoration.

worse, with fakes made to order in Paris. Let it simply be said that there is no concrete evidence for these charges, and the majority of archaeologists reject them. At the time of this writing in 2000, the great shaft grave treasures are located in the main ground-floor room, directly opposite the entrance, but there are plans to move some of these objects to a new museum directly on the site of Mycenae itself, in which case a study of the treasures will be part of a visit to the site.

From the National Archaeological Museum, the true Schliemann enthusiast will wish to visit the Schliemann family mausoleum in the first cemetery of Athens, another neoclassical building that resembles an ancient temple. A sculptured frieze around the supporting podium depicts Heinrich and Sophia in heroic poses at their excavations.

A visit to the magnificent Gennadeion Library of the American School of Classical Studies at 54 Souidias Street near Kolonaki Square in Athens would be a pleasant last stop, especially for those whose tastes run to scholarly pursuits and old books. Here are kept Schliemann's original excavation notebooks, diaries, and other important papers. These are carefully preserved as national treasures, and scholars from around the world come to study them. From time to time, some of them are exhibited to the public.

Schliemann's published books may be examined in the Gennadeion, a public library. Schliemann's monumental publications *Mycenae* and *Tiryns* would provide valuable background preparation for the rest of the tour. Most of Schliemann's publications have been translated into English and are available in major public and university libraries. Used copies appear frequently on Internet Web sites devoted to the used-book trade. Anyone with the chance to study original copies of Schliemann's publications, at home or in Athens, will note the excellent drawings and maps that illustrate them. They are admirable works of scholarship, and the quality of draftsmanship and book production was very high (Schliemann himself paid for them). The original first editions have beautiful bindings decorated with motifs copied from significant artifacts discovered in the excavations.

These books are very much part of our own active research library today. We well recall using them when we were students at the American School of Classical Studies in Athens in the 1970s. The school copies came with dedicatory inscriptions by the man himself, and it gave us a considerable thrill to know that we were using a book that was once handled by the great Schliemann.

Following the Schliemann Trail

The Schliemann trail is a long one, and in the following pages we offer suggestions for two tours, one short and the other for diehard Schliemann fans with plenty of time and no budget contraints. The short tour outside Athens begins at Nafplion in the Argolid, which served as Schliemann's base, and includes the sites of Mycenae and Tiryns. The diehard tour includes Ithaca, Knossos, Orchomenos, and Marathon, all of which are in Greece. A complete tour should include Troy in northwestern Turkey.

Let us begin with Nafplion. Schliemann based himself in this charming old town, which in its turn was the capital of Venetian Greece (when it was called Napoli di Romania), the seat of a pasha in the Ottoman period, and the first capital of independent Greece from 1831 until 1835, when Otho, the first king of the Hellenes, moved his residence to Athens. Nafplion is the most centrally located, convenient, and pleasant place to stay. Schliemann stayed at the Grand Bretannia Hotel (now defunct, but the building remains on the harbor front with a conspicuous sign). Today there are many other small and large hotels.

When Schliemann excavated at Tiryns (four kilometers from Nafplion) in the 1880s, he habitually took a swim in the bay at 4:00 A.M. (not recommended) and then rode his horse along the bay before turning inland to the site. Eucalyptus trees line the avenue from the bay to Tiryns. A popular story, passed from student to student, is that Schliemann planted them to provide shade for his daily ride to the site.

The site of Tiryns is easily reached by car following Schliemann's route, or one can take the modern highway from Nafplion to Argos that passes directly under the walls of the site. Buses and taxis are inexpensive alternatives to renting a car. Tiryns is well laid out for tourists; a guidebook is sold at the ticket kiosk, and plans and explanatory placards are posted in the ruins themselves.

The site is small enough to see in half a day; a longer visit could include the tholos tomb in the nearby hill of Profitis Elias (the guards at Tiryns can provide directions). The principal features are the great Cyclopean fortification walls and the remains of a megaron-style palace on the highest part of the hill. The palace, other outbuildings on the citadel's summit, and the vaulted galleries were the focus of Schliemann's excavations.

From the citadel one can see the so-called Lower Town directly to the west of the palace and enclosed by an extension of the fortification walls. The excavations here were undertaken in the 1970s and 1980s by a team from the German Archaeological Institute led by the late Klaus Kilian. The plain outside of the fortified citadel was the site of a much larger town. The town is now under about five meters of alluvium, but was detected by the geoarchaeologist Eberhard Zangger in a drilling program. The town was buried by flood deposits washed in by a stream that was subsequently diverted by a dam (ca. 1250 B.C.) to flow into a massive canal, which still redirects water-borne sediments into the bay of Nafplion. Today, this Mycenaean engineering requires the Port Authority of Nafplion to continually dredge the harbor in order to keep it clear for shipping.

When Schliemann excavated at Mycenae (20 kilometers from Nafplion) he stayed at the Belle Helene Hotel, which is still in business. Whether one stays at the site or returns to Nafplion for the night, the site of Mycenae should take an entire day to study. In addition to the fortified citadel with the Shaft Grave Circle A excavated by Schliemann, the Lion Gate, remains of a palace, and the hidden cistern, tholos tombs line the approach road to the site.

The largest and most impressive tholos tomb is the Treasury of Atreus, which looked much as it does today when Schliemann began his work. The smaller tholos, called the Tomb of Klytemnestra, is located near the Lion Gate, below the level of the tourist walkway. It was originally excavated and reconstructed under the direct supervision of Sophia Schliemann, her most lasting contribution to the archaeology of this site. Additional items of interest are the Shaft Grave Circle B discovered by George Papadimitriou and George Mylonas in the 1950s, the great houses opposite the Treasury of Atreus, which were excavated by the British archaeologist Alan Wace, and the bridge of Cyclopean masonry that marks the line of an ancient Mycenaean road leading to Tiryns. All of these features can be studied by walking the approach road from the modern village to the site.

If the new museum on the site is open, it should be visited, and on

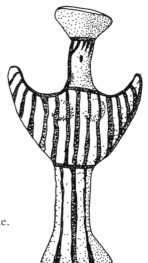

B.3 A terra-cotta figurine from Mycenae.

no account should one miss the chance to follow the road past the museum and walk up into the hills behind the site. Not only is this the beginning of a major Mycenaean road leading eastward from the site into the interior of the Argolid (several ancient bridges are still visible along its length), but it provides a magnificent view back to the citadel and the Argive plain beyond. On a clear day it is an excellent vantage point for taking photographs.

Back in Nafplion, the small archaeological museum is a memorable highlight. It is housed in the central square of the old town (Plateia Syntagmatos) in a beautiful early-eighteenth-century Venetian building and contains a wealth of finds from the new excavations at Mycenae and Tiryns. Although these materials are not directly connected with Schliemann, they are important and interesting. On display are figurines of worshipers (or gods?) from the House with the Idols, a cult center in the citadel of Mycenae discovered by Greek and British excavators in the 1960s, and a full suit of bronze armor from a chamber tomb at Dendra discovered in the 1950s by Swedish archaeologists. This last piece gives one a sense of the sophisticated weaponry of the Mycenaean warriors, which was no doubt a major reason for their success and wealth.

Having successfully concluded the tour of the Argolid, and with visions of the Lion Gate and the Tirynthian walls still fresh, this is the time to move on to Troy and the Istanbul Archaeological Museum, where finds from the new Trojan excavations are exhibited.

Troy

Prehistoric Troy has been excavated four times. Schliemann began the tradition in the 1870s and 1880s, and his former assistant Wilhelm Dörpfeld followed suit in the 1890s. Excavations were resumed in the 1930s by an American team under the direction of Carl Blegen of the University of Cincinnati, and full-scale excavation was undertaken again after 1988 by Manfred Korfmann and a team from Tübingen University in Germany and Brian Rose of the University of Cincinnati. Each excavation had different objectives. Schliemann explored an unknown site, in search of the Troy of the Homeric poems, which he associated at first with Troy II (ca. 2500 B.C.), the second settlement of nine at the site, when counted up from the bottom. After Schliemann's death in 1890, Dörpfeld concentrated his efforts on the investigation of Troy VI (ca. 1250 B.C.), which he regarded as the greatest of the nine settlements that occupy the mound of Hisarlik (the modern name of the site) and most likely the Homeric city. Blegen's excavations were concerned more with refining the stratigraphy and dating the site in order to clarify the Homeric associations than it was with making spectacular discoveries. Blegen complicated our understanding of the site by pinpointing Troy VIIa as the settlement associated with the Homeric Trojan War. The disagreement over the correct Homeric identification (Troy II, VI, or VIIa?) has been a source of much controversy for the past 50 years.

The modern excavations by Korfmann have several goals: to clean up the old excavation trenches, to conserve and restore existing remains, and to clarify the stratigraphy and history of the site. Korfmann has once again focused attention on Troy VI as the probable Homeric city by finding evidence that the settlement of Troy VI was considerably larger than previously imagined, making it by far the largest and most prosperous settlement known in the Aegean world at the time of the Trojan War. Most scholars today agree with Korfmann that Dörpfeld's identification of Troy VI as Homer's Troy is correct.

The site has been thoroughly cleaned and restored and is more accessible than ever before. With the relevant remains from each level clearly visible and prominently labeled, it is possible to view all parts of the site. This is important, because Troy is a very complicated site with a long history of occupation. Without such restorations and efforts to promote self-guided tours of the site, a great deal of imagination would be required to see the city of Troy for the great Bronze Age center that was the focus of a famous war and historic events that led to the end of an entire age.

Troy sits at the edge of a plain in a strategically valuable position at the mouth of the Dardanelles strait, where it could control all of the traffic from the Mediterranean to the Black Sea and the passage by land from Asia into Europe. This is the secret of Troy's wealth and power.

From the site of Troy itself, it would be interesting to investigate the Trojan plain known since antiquity as the Troad. This alluvial plain is criss-crossed with features that may be canals and other artificial works that may once have connected the site to a harbor on the southwestern edge of the plain. Eberhard Zangger has argued that these artificial works and the size of the city demonstrate that Troy was no Bronze Age town but a powerful kingdom that controlled a large part of western Asia Minor and perhaps the Aegean Sea. After all the momentous events that took place on the plain of Troy, it is perhaps one of the greatest of Romantic pleasures to roam the Troad armed with a copy of Homer's poems and to relive one of the great shaping epics of the Western world.

From Istanbul, Troy can be reached by bus, rental car, or organized tour. It takes a full day to get there, and the better part of a day is required to view the ruins, so allow plenty of time. The Archaeological Museum in Istanbul is a vital part of the tour. One entire floor has been devoted to a newly designed exhibit of Trojan antiquities that illustrates in a chronological sequence the archaeological cultures that have occupied the site of Hisarlik. These artifacts illustrate the material culture of the ancient Trojans; also on view are the very artifacts excavated by Schliemann and deposited with the Ottoman authorities at the museum in accordance with his excavation permit.

Priam's Treasure, a treasure of gold, silver, and bronze made famous as Schliemann's greatest find at Troy, and which was once thought by Schliemann to be the proof that Troy II was the Homeric city, is in fact an Early Bronze Age treasure hoard from a thousand years earlier. It is in any case not in the Istanbul museum. Originally smuggled out of the Ottoman Empire by Schliemann, it was donated to the State Museum in Berlin, and it disappeared in 1945 when Berlin fell to the Soviet Union. The whereabouts of Priam's Treasure was long a mystery. We know now that it was taken by the Soviets at the end of the war to the Pushkin Museum in Moscow, and the great treasure has come out of hiding at long last. At the time of writing it is on display in Moscow, but its final disposition has not yet been decided. There are nevertheless enough pieces of metalwork and jewelry on display in Istanbul from other Trojan finds to give one an idea of the appearance and style of Priam's Treasure.

A typical National Tourist Organization of Greece promotional poster shows a picture of Mykonos, Santorini, or one of a hundred other places in the Cycladic islands. The tourist has a vision of whitewashed village houses with pastel domes on sunny islands in the turquoise waters of the Aegean. The houses perch on colorful rocks, bare of vegetation, and in the distance a clean sandy beach stretches away in lovely isolation, beckoning to the viewer.

These places do indeed exist, but Greece is so much more! This whitewashed vision of Greece may hold for some areas, but its use in the ceaseless promotion of tourism comes at a cost. What is sacrificed? Greece is equally the fantastic sight of golden eagles drifting above spring meadows rich in wildflowers in the mountains of Epirus, Arcadia, or Crete; the lovely mountain villages of Mount Pelion with their towering, painted facades; and the rich cultural life of the great cities of Athens and Thessaloniki. The tourist posters and advertising art may capture parts of Greece, but like all symbolic representation, only by ignoring background and context.

The best times to travel in Greece are the spring and the autumn, but most people's schedules require them to visit Greece in the summer. Our experiences have mostly been summer ones too, because we are bound by an academic calendar that leaves only the months of June, July, and August (and sometimes the end of May) for field expeditions. Greece in the summer tends to be hot and sunny during the day, and slightly cooler in most areas in the evenings (especially in the mountains, of course). It rains very little.

Greek cities have all the features of European centers—historic centers, museums, art galleries, and shopping malls that cater to every taste and budget. Because of the heat, afternoon naptime used to be strictly observed. Everyone ate a big lunch about 3:00 P.M., then napped until 5:30 or 6:00. For those still awake, it was the quietest, most serene time of the day. We write in the past tense because in today's more modern Greece the hustle and bustle of the mechanized world seems to keep many people, especially young city people, from their naps. Nevertheless, most businesses and government offices still close for several hours in the afternoon. Tourists should plan to transact necessary business, like cashing travelers checks, in the morning. In most places, stores reopen in the evening, on certain days. The days on which this happens vary from community to community.

In the next section, we provide a few suggestions for traveling comfortably amidst mosquitoes, noise, heat, and too much sun. However, the positive aspects of traveling in Greece far outweigh these minor summer nuisances. What appeals to us (with our prehistoric minds) is the friendliness of the Greeks, the slow pace of life, and the small scale of the houses, shops, and streets (which are sometimes staircases for donkeys) that constitute the rural towns and villages. We are attracted to the old buildings and the traditional ways still followed in places. Although garbage is increasingly found on city streets, beside the roads, and in the sea, the country's great natural beauty predominates. The turquoise and azure sea water is clear, the mountains are majestic mounds of hazy blue, and the red, yellow, and pink flowers next to the whitewashed houses and against the clear blue sky provide a visual feast. The stillness of the olive groves filled with cicadas in the hot afternoon and the tiny village squares shaded with great plane trees are an environmental tonic for American city dwellers.

The climate and terrain vary from Mediterranean to alpine. The southern regions of Attica, the Peloponnese, Euboia, and the Cyclades and Crete are typically Mediterranean, with hot dry summers and cool rainy winters. Without frosts, the olive and the vine, bougainvillea and other delicate flowers thrive, and people enjoy the rainless summer weather. In these semiarid lands only scrub vegetation and isolated stands of evergreen oaks and pines survive outside cultivated areas.

In the northern areas of Thessaly, Macedonia, and Thrace, the countryside opens up into great fertile plains with a more continental, temperate climate that brings snow and cold in the winter and great heat in the summer. Western Greece is separated from the east by chains of mountains, the Pindos in the north and Arcadia in the Peloponnese. Because of the prevailing storm patterns, the western provinces are well watered and have more vegetation; they are the garden spots of Greece.

There are significant mountainous areas, particularly in the north-central part of the country. The highest areas supported glaciers in the last Ice Age and today shelter snow fields well into June. The mountains harbor fir and deciduous oak and are dotted with picturesque villages built of weathered gray stone; some are constructed high on pedestals with great overhanging balconies in the Ottoman fashion. The residents of these regions (Pindos, Arcadia, Zagoria, and Pelion) were once primarily shepherds and merchants, producers of cheese, yogurt, meat, and woolen textiles. Their mountains are rich in flowers and birds, and sky-blue rivers jet through deep canyons overarched by ancient stone bridges.

These regions of alpine Greece have distinctive architectural and artistic traditions, now artfully displayed in many regional village museums. They are noted also for their rich cuisine of bean soups, sausage stews, and country "pitas," baked pastries of filo dough with fillings of sausage, cheese, wild greens, and other savory things.

City or country, mountain or sea, mainland or island, all of these are Greece. To visit Athens, Delphi, Olympia, and Santorini, with an excursion to Crete or Rhodes, a route followed by millions of pilgrims and tourists, and to say you have "seen Greece" is tantamount to visiting the Boston Common, Manhattan, and the Mall in Washington, D.C. (with an excursion to San Diego?), and saying you have seen America. Dare to go off the beaten track, take the side roads, head inland from the beaches, and be rewarded!

Traditional mountain architecture can be seen in such places as Makrynitsa and Portaria on Mount Pelion near Volos, and traditional costumes are still to be spotted in the village of Metsovo in the Pindos mountains or on some islands (such as Lefkas). Fine ethnographic museums exist in Metsovo, Nafplion, Ioannina, Melos, Athens, and many other localities. Breathtaking natural beauty, along with mountain trekking, is available in the Vikos Gorge region north of Ioannina and in the Tayegetos Mountain district near Sparta. Some of the Greek islands, such as Andros and Spetses, are less frequented than others and have fine examples of traditional architecture. Tourists who also want good beaches might try the coast north of Preveza in Epirus, the western Peloponnese, or the Chalkidiki instead of the heavily visited beaches of the Cycladic islands. All of these areas and much more await the traveler with time, transport, and a desire to get away from the most heavily visited tourist centers.

What to Take to Greece: The Essentials

Greece has plenty of mosquitoes, but a spraying program at the end of World War II eliminated malaria. Nevertheless, mosquitoes are still a nuisance, so be prepared. Carry a stick of repellent in the evening to apply to ankles and ears while dining outdoors. Most homes and hotels do not have window and door screens. We take some netting with us in our suitcase (it folds up into a very small packet and weighs nothing) and some push pins. A piece of fine-mesh netting like that used for bridal veils, 2–3 yards long and 60 inches wide, adapts to any hotel room situation from sliding balcony doors to shuttered windows. We prefer the netting to the chemical fumes from mosquito repellents. Although more and more hotels are air-conditioned, many turn the cool air off in the middle of the night, making it necessary to open the windows.

Greece is noisy wherever people cluster. Greek settlement patterns, personal space requirements, and noise tolerances are different from American ones. Houses and apartments are packed tightly together in cities, of course, but the same pattern prevails in smaller communities as well. Even villagers hear their neighbors' conversations and televisions at night because they have their windows and doors open. Streets and roads are winding and narrow between the houses and villages; those that are too narrow for cars are no problem for motor scooters and motorcycles. Greeks tend to stay up half the night eating, talking, driving, and watching TV. So if you want to go to bed before midnight and get some uninterrupted sleep, use ear plugs.

Particularly now, with the ozone layer disintegrating, it is important to protect yourself from the strong Greek sun while visiting archaeological sites, swimming, and enjoying the scenery. A hat is a must. Choose a light-colored one with a wide brim and a secure fastener so that it will not blow off in the strong summer tradewinds. Long sleeves are a good idea, but liquid sun block can be substituted. If you elect to wear long sleeves, pick a light-colored cotton shirt.

It is difficult not to be identified as a tourist, but if you do not want to stand out in a crowd, do what the Greeks do. Greek men do not usually wear shorts in the city, but they don them when in vacation mode near the sea. Likewise, Greek women generally wear skirts or dresses in the city but are more casual in the country. Hardly anyone wears a sports coat or suit and tie in the summer. For cool evenings, we recommend a sweater or a light jacket. Rain can come in any month but is rare in the summer (although more common in northern and western Greece). Because rain showers are usually brief, carrying an umbrella is not worth the trouble. But a small folding rain poncho that fits in a purse or pocket is useful in an emergency.

For almost every occasion, we wear sandals, except when visiting archaeological sites or hiking in the countryside. On those occasions, good shoes that grip the rocky trails and support the ankles are a necessity. Be forewarned that you will not encounter smooth walkways at any archaeological sites you visit, only uneven rocky trails with loose and sometimes well-worn and slippery rocks.

Getting Around

Apart from organized bus tours, transport in Greece can be done by public bus, plane, train, and private car. The transport system is modern, efficient, safe, and reasonably priced. We have found, however, that our vagabonding habits are best served by having a private car. Despite the high price of renting, the convenience and the time saved are worth the cost, especially for getting to areas not easily reached by public transportation. If you wish to explore and time is short, a rental car is the best investment.

Driving is always an adventure, and in Greece, it is an *exciting* adventure not for the timid or weak of heart. Driving customs and regulations are similar to those in all parts of Europe. An international driver's license from the American Automobile Association and a credit card are required to rent a car. Athens is the main center for rental cars. The best-known rental-car agencies also have offices in the larger regional towns (Thessaloniki, Iraklion, Patras, and others).

A good road map is recommended. Road signs are plentiful, and every town and village is clearly marked with a sign in Greek and Latin letters, but trips should be carefully planned. Although Greece is very small (about the size of the state of Alabama) and distances are short, driving times can be longer than expected because road conditions are poor, there are no freeways (to speak of), and the traffic can be heavy. Even the main national roads go through towns and villages, some of which are choked with local traffic in narrow streets. So you must allow plenty of time to get from one place to another and should allow about twice as much time to your destination as you would expect on the basis of the mileage alone. Remember also that Greece is very mountainous and many roads have very steep grades; if you get behind a truck or a bus the going can be very slow.

The national road between Athens and Patras is wide, new, and very fast, as are bits and pieces of the main artery north from Athens to Thessaloniki. Everywhere else there are small, narrow two-lane asphalt roads without shoulders of any kind. These roads are often poorly engineered, badly maintained, and almost wholly unmarked (or sometimes marked in a confusing or misleading way). For instance, one sharp curve or steep drop-off may be marked with an exclamation point or reduced-speed signs, and the next one, two or three kilometers on, will have no indication of danger at all. We guess they have considered you to be forewarned after the first signs.

Greek drivers are very aggressive and they drive fast. But despite the seeming traffic anarchy, particularly in the cities, there is a system. And it is important to know that cars in Greece are expensive and highly valued prestige items. No driver wants to scratch or dent his car, and some care is taken to avoid collision.

Beware of rough or irregular surfaces at all times, especially when it begins to rain. Drive more slowly than the posted speed limit, and be prepared to slow down at the least sign of difficulty. It is not advisable to drive at night because of poor road conditions. You must expect to find virtually anything in the road right around the corner, even on the best of roads. Exercise extreme care, particularly in villages where children play in the streets. In our years of driving, we have experienced all of the following at unexpected points in the road: snakes, tortoises, cats, dogs, chickens, mules, donkeys, horses, cows, sheep, goats, men, women, children, pushcarts, wagons, tractors, bicycles, broken-down vehicles, military tanks, fallen rocks, landslides, and a bewildering miscellany of debris, from bricks to appliances to huge marble blocks. And these obstacles were all on the *main* roads. The side roads can be even trickier.

Language

The official language is Demotic Greek, which is considerably different in grammar and vocabulary from Ancient Greek. A solid grounding in the Greek alphabet and familiarity with a Berlitz guide will help the visitor to make out shop signs, advertisements, and newspaper headlines, but is not strictly necessary. All important signs, directions, displays, and most menus are accompanied by Latin letter transliterations, and typically a French or English translation as well. English is the language of tourism and is widely recognized in hotels, restaurants, shops, car rental offices, and museums. We have never known a monolingual tourist to have difficulty communicating while on holiday in Greece.

We urge you strongly, however, to get a phrase book and do some cramming before you go. Most Greeks are friendly and extroverted and will happily converse with strangers via sign language if all else fails. They know their language is difficult and that few tourists speak it. But if you learn even a few simple phrases such as *kalimera sas* (good-day, or hello), *parakalo* (please), and *efharisto* (thank you), the average Greek in the street will be flattered and pleased and all the more eager to engage in conversation. So don't be afraid to give it a try; the Greeks will appreciate your effort.

Bibliographic Essay

The literature on the prehistoric archaeology of Greece is not particularly large, but it does span a century and includes everything from highly technical journal articles communicating data to a small number of specialists to student textbooks and books intended for a huge general audience. The sources listed here are some of the most useful and interesting works, chiefly those we consulted for this book. The list is not comprehensive, but only a small selection. Most are widely available in academic libraries and good municipal libraries, or can be ordered through interlibrary loan departments, bookstores, or the Internet. We have cited the editions that we consulted personally, and many of the older works can be found in later reprintings. The literature on Greek prehistory is written in many languages, among which Greek, English, French, German, and Italian predominate, but we have listed English-language texts wherever possible. For readers who would like to dig a little deeper, we have included some key works in other languages.

CHAPTER ONE *An Introduction to the Prehistory of Greece*

Any book on Greek archaeology should start with the opening chapters of Thucydides' history of the Peloponnesian War. There are many translations of his works into English, beginning with Thomas Hobbes's of 1642, which was intended to head off the English Civil War. It failed to avert hostilities, but Hobbes's translation is still recommended for its forceful, Elizabethan style (Thomas Hobbes, trans., with notes and introduction by David Greene, *Thucydides: The Peloponnesian War* (Chicago: University of Chicago Press, 1989). The translation by Rex Warner, *Thucydides: History of the Peloponnesian War* (Harmondsworth, Eng.: Penguin, 1984), however, is widely available and a good place to start. The quotations in the text are from this edition: Book 1, chap. 22; and Book 3, chap. 84.

For readers desiring more general knowledge about the archaeology of Greece, several textbooks provide information about the preclassical age. Older texts and specialized literature are cited below under the headings for specific chapters, but the beginner may wish to start with the summaries in recent publications such as R. L. N. Barber's *The Cyclades in the Bronze Age* (London: Duckworth, 1987); Oliver Dickinson's *The Aegean Bronze Age* (Cambridge: Cambridge University Press, 1994); John Griffiths Pedley's *Greek Art and Archaeology* (Englewood Cliffs, N.J: Prentice Hall, 1993); and W. R. Biers's *The Archaeology of Greece* (Ithaca, N.Y.: Cornell University Press, 1987).

CHAPTER TWO   *The Old Stone Age*

The Old Stone Age (Palaeolithic) in Greece must be viewed on a wide canvas that includes the rest of the Balkans, Europe, the Near East, and Africa. To understand the significance of the finds in Greece it is important to know something about human evolution and to be familiar with the different hominids and the characteristic stone-tool cultures of the Palaeolithic period. A number of readily available books provide this background information. For fossil hominids, Richard Klein's *The Human Career* (Chicago: University of Chicago Press, 1999) is an up-to-date and authoritative textbook. Clive Gamble, in *The Palaeolithic Societies of Europe* (New York: Cambridge University Press, 1999), provides a good summary of the Palaeolithic in Europe. Specifically for the Neanderthals there are two excellent general books on the subject. One is Erik Trinkaus and Pat Shipman's *The Neanderthals: Changing the Image of Mankind* (London: Jonathan Cape, 1993), a very interesting history of the discovery and study of the Neanderthals. The other is Christopher Stringer and Clive Gamble's *In Search of the Neanderthals* (London: Thames and Hudson, 1993), which presents a comprehensive overview of the archaeology of the Neanderthals and related groups in Europe, with an emphasis on the vexed question of the replacement of the Neanderthals by early modern humans. For those who wish to delve deeply into the subject, the book by Paul Mellars, *The Neanderthal Legacy: An Archaeological Perspective from Western Europe* (Princeton, N.J.: Princeton University Press, 1996), is the latest statement on the subject by a noted authority.

The complexity of early Palaeolithic life in Europe can be glimpsed at the recently excavated site of Boxgrove in southern England. There the excavators found evidence of sophisticated tool use, cooperative hunting of large game such as rhinoceros, and even such subtle activities as the preparation of skins and the use of language, which is implied by cooperative action. The forward-thinking and planned behavior seen at Boxgrove are evident also in the careful placement of sites in the Greek landscape for resource exploitation. The Boxgrove excavations are fully described in Mark Roberts and Simon Parfitt's *Boxgrove: A Middle Pleistocene Hominid Site at Eartham Quarry, Boxgrove, West Sussex* (London: 1999) and a popular book by Michael Pitts and Mark Roberts, *Fairweather Eden* (New York: 1998).

A more technical summary of the evidence for the earlier Palaeolithic in Greece, which includes references to the scientific literature, is provided by Curtis Runnels in "The Stone Age of Greece from the Palaeolithic to the Advent of the Neolithic," *American Journal of Archaeology* 99 (1995): 699–728. A comprehensive overview of the Upper Palaeolithic is found in the substantial contributions of the Cambridge University team presented in a publication edited by Geoff Bailey, *Klithi: Palaeolithic Settlement and Quaternary Landscapes in Northwest Greece* (Cambridge: McDonald Institute for Archaelogical Research, 1997). For an overview of the impact of Pleistocene sea-level changes on the landscape of Greece and the people, animals, and plants that occupied it, see Tjeerd H. van Andel's "Late Quaternary Sea-Level Changes and Archaeology," *Antiquity* 63 (1989): 733–45; and Kurt Lambeck's "Sea-Level Change and Shore-Line Evolution in Aegean Greece Since Upper Palaeolithic Time," *Antiquity* 70 (1996): 588–611.

CHAPTER THREE   *The New Stone Age*

The first detailed summary of the Neolithic period came with the book by Demetrios Theocharis, *Neolithic Greece* (Athens: National Bank of Greece, 1973), which has been updated by George Papathanasopoulos, *The Neolithic Culture of Greece* (Athens: N. P. Goulandris Foundation, 1996). In the roughly 25 years between the publication of these two works, the field of Neolithic studies progressed so far that the Papathanasopoulos volume required the contributions of more than 25 specialists to cover the subject. Both volumes are very well illustrated. For succinct but detailed and technical summaries of the period by noted authorities, see articles by Jean-Paul Demoule and Catherine Perlès, "The Greek Neolithic: A New Review," *Journal of World Prehistory* 7 (1993): 355–416; and Stelios Andreou, Michael Fotiadis, and Kostas Kotsakis, "The Neolithic and Bronze Age of Northern Greece," *American Journal of Archaeology* 100 (1996): 537–97.

The subject of the origins of Neolithic culture in Greece, particularly the debate over indigenous development versus the arrival of immigrants from Anatolia, has a long history. An overview of the subject can be found in V. Gordon Childe's *What Happened in History* (Harmondsworth, Eng.: Penguin, 1985); Colin Renfrew's *Archaeology and Language: The Puzzle of Indo-European Origins* (New York: Cambridge University Press, 1987); and Tjeerd H. van Andel and Curtis N. Runnels's "The Earliest Farmers in Europe," *Antiquity* 69 (1995): 481–500. The case for indigenous development of agriculture in Greece is made by Robin Dennell in *European Economic Prehistory: A New Approach* (London: Academic Press, 1983), and a discussion of the Wave of Advance model and the case for the demic diffusion hypothesis can be found in Albert J. Ammerman and L. L. Cavalli-Sforza's *The Neolithic Transition and the Genetics of Populations in Europe* (Princeton, N.J.: Princeton University Press, 1984).

Evidence for seafaring Neolithic migrants is especially clear at the site of Knossos in Crete, the same place where the later Palace of Minos would rise, and this evidence is discussed by Cyprian Broodbank and Thomas F. Strasser in "Migrant Farmers and the Neolithic Colonization of Crete," *Antiquity* 65 (1991): 233–45. They stress the deliberate nature of the colonization of Crete, which was previously uninhabited and required repeated crossings of the Aegean Sea to bring the seed, animal stocks, and additional colonists necessary to make the project viable.

Franchthi Cave is arguably the most important site in Greece for study of the Stone Age, and any serious reader should investigate the evidence from this site firsthand. The results of the excavations have been published in a series of volumes by Indiana University Press under the general editorship of Thomas W. Jacobsen with the title *Excavations at Franchthi Cave, Greece*. Eleven volumes (called fascicles) have been published since 1987 (other volumes are in preparation), covering such diverse themes as the evolution of the landscape, marine shells, animal bones, stone tools, stratigraphy, pottery, and figurines. Although there is not yet any general survey of the excavation results, the summary by Tjeerd H. van Andel and Curtis Runnels in *Beyond the Acropolis: A Rural Greek Past* (Stanford, Calif.: Stanford University Press, 1987) will prove helpful before tackling the final excavation reports.

The effects of Neolithic settlement expansion on the Greek landscape are explored in a number of places ranging from the technical
to the more general. For the former, see the article by Tjeerd H. van
Andel, Eberhard Zangger, and Anne Demitrack, "Land Use and
Soil Erosion in Prehistoric and Historical Greece," *Journal of Field
Archaeology* 17 (1990): 379–96; for the latter, see Curtis Runnels's
"Environmental Degradation in Ancient Greece," *Scientific American*
272 (1995): 72–75. Oliver Rackham and Jennifer Moody provide an
interesting case study for one region of Greece in *The Making of the
Cretan Landscape* (Manchester, Eng.: Manchester University Press,
1996).

CHAPTER FOUR   *The Bronze Age*

The quotation at the beginning of the chapter is from Donald Greene,
ed., *Samuel Johnson* (Oxford: Oxford University Press, 1984), p. 624.
The rediscovery of the Greek Bronze Age cultures of Mycenae and
the Minoans is a fascinating subject, well covered by several recent
books, the best of which are J. Lesley Fitton's *The Discovery of the Greek
Bronze Age* (London: British Museum Press, 1995); and William A.
McDonald and Carol G. Thomas's *Progress into the Past: The Rediscovery of Mycenaean Civilization* (Bloomington: Indiana University Press,
1990). The position of the Mycenaean-Minoan world in the Mediterranean world can be appreciated by perusing the old but still readable handbook by V. Gordon Childe, *Man Makes Himself* (London:
Watts, 1939). General textbooks for the period include the books
by Barber and Dickinson (listed in the Bibliographic Essay for Chapter One). To their number we would add a newer study of one of
the Mycenaean kingdoms by excavation and survey, Jack L. Davis,
ed., *Sandy Pylos: An Archaeological History from Nestor to Navarino*
(Austin: University of Texas Press, 1998). Bronze Age material culture
for all periods is described and illustrated in a number of useful hand-
books, among which the best are by Reynold Higgins, *Minoan and
Mycenaean Art* (New York: Thames and Hudson, 1985); and Sinclair
Hood, *The Arts in Prehistoric Greece* (New York: Penguin, 1978).

Early Bronze Age civilization in the Aegean as a whole is also covered by the groundbreaking book by Colin Renfrew, *The Emergence
of Civilization* (London: Methuen, 1972). An update on Renfrew's important work is given in Tjeerd H. van Andel and Curtis N. Runnels's
"An Essay on the 'Emergence of Civilization' in the Aegean World,"

Antiquity 62 (1988): 234–47. For readers with a serious itch to know the latest findings and interpretations in the field of Bronze Age archaeology, the reviews of Aegean prehistory published by the *American Journal of Archaeology* with support from the Institute for Aegean Prehistory are valuable resources. This important series of papers was written by experts in the field and gives an up-to-date overview of the subject from region to region. These papers have been updated and reprinted recently in a single volume. For the Early Bronze Age on the mainland, see Jeremy B. Rutter's "The Prepalatial Bronze Age of the Southern and Central Greek Mainland," *American Journal of Archaeology* 97 (1993): 745–97. The islands are covered by Jack L. Davis in "The Islands of the Aegean," *American Journal of Archaeology* 96 (1992): 699–756. Those with a serious interest in the archaeology of Minoan Crete will find two articles in this series of particular value, Paul Rehak and John G. Younger's "Neopalatial, Final Palatial, and Postpalatial Crete," *American Journal of Archaeology* 102 (1998): 91–173, which covers the periods of the great palaces; and L. Vance Watrous's "Crete from the Earliest Prehistory Through the Protopalatial Period," *American Journal of Archaeology* 98 (1994): 695–753. Mainland Greece in the Mycenaean age is covered by Cynthia W. Shelmerdine in "The Palatial Bronze Age of the Southern and Central Greek Mainland," *American Journal of Archaeology* 101 (1997): 537–85. For northern Greece in the Bronze Age, see the article by Andreou, Fotiadis, and Kotsakis cited for Chapter Three.

General introductions to Minoan Crete are numerous and offer a good place to start one's reading about this civilization before advancing to more specialized works. Among the most widely available are Reynold Higgins's *The Archaeology of Minoan Crete* (London: Bodley Head, 1973); H. E. L. Mellersh's *Minoan Crete* (New York: Putnam, 1967); R. W. Hutchinson's *Prehistoric Crete* (Baltimore: Pelican, 1962); and Rodney Castleden's *Minoans: Life in Bronze Age Crete* (London: Routledge, 1993).

Many specialized contributions to the literature will be of use to the serious student and all visitors to Crete. The following guides to the Minoan palaces are essential for understanding these complex sites: Gerald Cadogan's *Palaces of Minoan Crete* (London: Methuen, 1976); and J. W. Graham's *The Palaces of Crete* (Princeton, N.J.: Princeton University Press, 1987). The results of the first 50 years of excavation are admirably summarized and illustrated by J. D. S. Pendlebury in *The Archaeology of Crete: An Introduction* (London: Methuen, 1939).

The vast subject of Minoan religion can be approached through Nanno Marinatos's *Minoan Religion: Ritual, Image, and Symbol* (Columbia: University of South Carolina Press, 1993). A widely available and lovely book detailing the excavation of one of the Minoan palaces is by Nicholas Platon, *Zakros: The Discovery of a Lost Palace of Ancient Crete* (New York: Scribner's, 1971). The theory that the Palace of Minos at Knossos continued as a seat of Mycenaean power until the late thirteenth century was first advanced by Leonard R. Palmer in *Mycenaeans and Minoans* (New York: Knopf, 1963). Finally, the articles by Rehak, Younger, and Watrous cited above should be consulted for recent findings and interpretations.

The Mycenaeans of the mainland have been the subject of several recent publications, among which is Lord William Taylour's *The Mycenaeans* (London: Thames and Hudson, 1984); see also the wonderfully crafted introduction by Emily Vermeule in *Greece in the Bronze Age* (Chicago: University of Chicago Press, 1964). Vermeule's short chapters on the Stone Age are now badly out of date, but her comments on the Shaft Grave Circles at Mycenae and other aspects of Mycenaean culture, particularly the difficulties of understanding Linear B, are well worth careful study. The decipherment of Linear B, one of the great intellectual triumphs of Aegean archaeology, is ably covered in two widely available books by John Chadwick: *The Decipherment of Linear B* (Cambridge: Cambridge University Press, 1958) and *Linear B and Related Scripts* (Berkeley: University of California Press, 1987). A later work by John Chadwick, *The Mycenaean World* (Cambridge: Cambridge University Press, 1976), makes extensive use of the Linear B tablets to supplement other evidence and to round out the picture of Mycenaean agriculture, social structure, agriculture, economy, and warfare. Other general introductions to the Mycenaeans and specific sites include: Alan E. Samuel's *The Mycenaeans in History* (Englewood Cliffs, N.J.: Prentice Hall, 1966); George Mylonas's *Ancient Mycenae* (Princeton, N.J.: Princeton University Press, 1957); Joseph Alsop's *From the Silent Earth* (New York: Harper and Row, 1964); and J. T. Hooker's *Mycenaean Greece* (London: Routledge and Kegan Paul, 1976). The most comprehensive summary of the destructions that overwhelmed the Mycenaean world is by Per Ålin in *Das Ende der Mykenischen Fundstätten auf dem Griechischen Festland* (Lund, Sweden: Carl Bloms, 1962).

Surveys that have tested settlement patterns in the Argolid include those by James C. Wright et al., "The Nemea Valley Archaeological Project: A Preliminary Report," *Hesperia* 59 (1990): 579–659; Michael H. Jameson, Curtis N. Runnels, and Tjeerd H. van Andel, *A Greek Countryside: The Southern Argolid from Prehistory to the Present Day* (Stanford, Calif.: Stanford University Press, 1995); Berit Wells, Curtis Runnels, and Eberhard Zangger, "The Berbati-Limnes Archaeological Survey: The 1988 Season," *Opuscula Atheniensia* 18 (1990): 207–38; and Berit Wells and Curtis Runnels, eds., *The Berbati-Limnes Archaeological Survey 1988–1990* (Stockholm: Swedish Institute, 1996).

CHAPTER FIVE   *The End of the Bronze Age World*

The role of natural disasters in the breakup of the Bronze Age Aegean world was first broached by Rhys Carpenter in *Discontinuity in Greek Civilization* (Cambridge: Cambridge University Press, 1966) and has been discussed more recently by Eberhard Zangger in two books, *The Geoarchaeology of the Argolid* (Berlin: Mann, 1993), and *The Flood from Heaven: Deciphering the Atlantis Legend* (London: Sidgwick and Sackson, 1992). Useful summaries of the problems associated with the end of the Mycenaean world in specific and the Bronze Age world in general are found in Taylour, *The Mycenaeans* (cited for Chapter Four), and N. K. Sandars, *The Sea Peoples* (London: Thames and Hudson, 1978). An article by Philip Betancourt, "The End of the Greek Bronze Age," *Antiquity* 50 (1976): 40–77, offers a thorough summary of all the arguments and can be taken as an example of the "systems collapse" school of cultural catastrophe. All of the theories are thoroughly reviewed and critiqued by Robert Drews in *The End of the Bronze Age: Changes in Warfare and the Catastrophe ca. 1200 B.C.* (Princeton, N.J.: Princeton University Press, 1993), as a prelude to the introduction of a new theory of cultural collapse. Leon Pomerance's ideas were published in *The Final Collapse of Thera (Santorini)* (Lund, Sweden: Carl Bloms, 1970).

We predict that attempts to find natural explanations for the Bronze Age catastrophe are unlikely to go away. Amos Nur of the Department of Earth Sciences at Stanford University, for instance, has given new life to the earthquake theory by postulating that there were periodic seismic "storms" that brought clusters of earthquakes to the region resulting in larger scale and more thoroughgoing destruction (Amos Nur, personal communication, 1998).

The topic of the excavations at Troy is endlessly fascinating because of its connections with the Homeric poems. For an overview of the first three archaeological expeditions to Troy, see Carl W. Blegen's *Troy and the Trojans* (New York: Praeger, 1963); and Michael Wood's *In Search of the Trojan War* (Berkeley: University of California Press, 1998). The new expedition to Troy, begun in 1989, is being described in a series of illustrated volumes under the general editorship of Manfred Korfmann with the title *Studia Troica* (Mainz am Rhein: Von Zabern, 1991–).Contributions are in German, English, and other languages. The well-illustrated and handsomely produced volumes provide a sweeping overview of the whole subject. A home page on the World Wide Web presents recent updates and reports of ongoing research at the site: *http://ucaswww.mcm.uc.edu/classics/troy*. Most researchers believe that the Turkish site of Hisarlik is the actual site of Homeric Troy, but some dissent exists; a different view is clearly laid out in a famous essay by Sir Moses Finley, "Schliemann's Troy—One Hundred Years After," in M. I. Finley, *The World of Odysseus* (New York: Viking, 1978), pp. 159–77.

The rather mysterious Sea Peoples, who are often invoked in connection with the catastrophic close of the Mediterranean Bronze Age, are the subject of N. K. Sandars's *The Sea Peoples* (cited above) and Eberhard Zangger's *Ein Neuer Kampf um Troia* (Munich: Droemer Knaur, 1994). The evidence for the rather surprising conclusion, at least on first telling, that the biblical Philistines are none other than mainland Mycenaean Greeks arriving on the shores of today's Palestine as part of the migrations of Sea Peoples, and giving it its common name, is set out in detail by Trude and Moshe Dothan in *People of the Sea: The Search for the Philistines* (New York: Macmillan, 1992).

CHAPTER SIX   *Santorini and the Legend of Atlantis*

The modern legend of Atlantis was set in motion and given lasting direction by Ignatius Donnelly in *Atlantis: The Antediluvian World* (New York: Harper and Brothers, 1882). The connection between Atlantis, Minoan Crete, and Akrotiri (Santorini, also known as Thera) has been discussed in a number of books, including those by A. G. Galanopoulos and Edward Bacon, *Atlantis: The Truth Behind the Legend* (Indianapolis: Bobbs-Merrill, 1969); and James W. Mavor Jr., *Voyage to Atlantis* (New York: Putnam, 1969). A good summary of what we know about Akrotiri can be found in Christos G. Doumas's *Thera: Pompeii of the Ancient Aegean* (London: Thames and Hudson, 1983). Anyone seriously interested in the Atlantis legend should begin by reading Plato's original account of Atlantis in his dialogues, *Critias* and *Timaeus* in the translation by R. G. Bury, *The Loeb Classical Library: Plato* (Cambridge, Mass.: Harvard University Press, 1981). Scholarly evaluations of the Atlantis legend include those by Edwin S. Ramage, ed., *Atlantis Fact or Fiction?* (Bloomington: Indiana University Press, 1978); Dorothy B. Vitaliano, *Legends of the Earth* (Bloomington: Indiana University Press, 1973); and Eberhard Zangger's *The Flood from Heaven* (cited for Chapter 5). The contributions of geologists, volcanologists, seismologists, and archaeologists to our understanding of the Minoan Eruption of Santorini can be followed in the proceedings of three international conferences, the last and most useful of which has been published in three fat volumes edited by D. A. Hardy et al., *Thera and the Aegean World III* (London: Thera Foundation, 1990).

CHAPTER SEVEN   *A Tour of the Principal Monuments*
                of Prehistoric Greece

There are no useful guidebooks for prehistoric Greece as there are for the later Bronze Age, but perhaps it is not out of place to suggest a novel? The mystery by Hammond Innes, *Levkas Man* (New York: Knopf, 1971), is still widely available and is a pleasant read. The American School of Classical Studies at Athens produced a small guide to the site of Lerna and its antiquities by John L. Caskey and E. T. Blackburn, *Lerna in the Argolid* (Princeton, N.J.: Princeton University Press, 1997).

The studies of pottery and the social conclusions drawn from them can be sampled in Tracey Cullen's "Social Implications of Ceramic Style in the Neolithic Peloponnese," in W. D. Kingery, ed., *Ancient Technology to Modern Science* (Columbus: American Ceramic Society, 1985), pp. 77–100; and Karen D. Vitelli's "Were Pots First Made for Foods? Doubts from Franchthi," *World Archaeology* 21 (1989): 17–29.

On the whimsical side we recommend Gregory Benford's *Artifact* (New York: Eos, 1998), for light reading in connection with a trip to Nafplion and the Argolid. It is a science-fiction thriller about world-shattering discoveries made by archaeologists from our own Department of Archaeology at Boston University somewhere "south of Nafplion" (i.e., in the vicinity of Franchthi Cave). We assure readers that we and our colleagues do not have strange alien devices secreted in our departmental storage areas, and almost never have as much excitement in a lifetime as Mr. Benford manages to pack into a single day of the fictional life of an archaeologist. The book is fun to read nevertheless.

CHAPTER EIGHT *Last Reflections*

For Friedrich Nietzsche on the will to power, see Walter Kaufmann, translator, *On the Genealogy of Morals and Ecce Homo* (New York: Vintage, 1969). Arnold Toynbee attempts to explain history in *A Study of History* (New York: Oxford University Press, 1947); and Oswald Spengler famously characterizes the birth, growth, maturity, and death of civilizations in *The Decline of the West* (New York: Knopf, 1932). The concept of the coevolution of landscape and human settlement in prehistoric Greece is discussed in more detail by M. H. Jameson, C. N. Runnels, and T. H. van Andel in *A Greek Countryside: The Southern Argolid from Prehistory to the Present Day* (Stanford, Calif.: Stanford University Press, 1994), pp. 324–414. Charles Redman provides one example of the modern tendency to explain the evolution of ancient civilizations as processes divorced from individual actions or grand causal schemes in *The Rise of Civilization: From Early Farmers to Urban Society in the Ancient Near East* (San Francisco: Freeman, 1978).

The literature on ancient civilizations is growing rapidly, and only a few titles on this subject can be mentioned. For a recent and very sophisticated view of the rise of civilizations, see Bruce G. Trigger's *Early Civilizations: Ancient Egypt in Context* (Cairo: American University in Cairo Press, 1996). The collapse of civilizations has been treated in detail by Joseph A. Tainter in *The Collapse of Complex Societies* (Cambridge: Cambridge University Press, 1990); and by Norman Yoffee and George L. Cowgill, eds., in *The Collapse of Ancient States and Civilizations* (Tucson: University of Arizona Press, 1988).

The Romantic view of Greece as an unchanging landscape once inhabited by the worthy ancients on which the modern natives carry on the way of life and embody the same values as their ancient forebears is a complex and very interesting subject. An early and still valuable study is T. J. B. Spencer's *Fair Greece! Sad Relic: Literary Philhellenism from Shakespeare to Byron* (London: Weidenfeld and Nicolson, 1954). The quintessential traveler's view of the ancient Mediterranean as viewed from the Romantic perspective is Dame Rose Macaulay's *Pleasure of Ruins* (London: Weidenfeld and Nicolson, 1953). The Romantic view of European and American travelers to Greece may be found in a fascinating book by Robert Eisner, *Travelers to an Antique Land: The History and Literature of Travel to Greece* (Ann Arbor: University of Michigan Press, 1991), which is a travel book about travel books. Two other books on this subject are essential reading: Hugh Tregakis, in *Beyond the Grand Tour: The Levant Lunatics* (London: Ascent, 1979), gives short biographies of some of the earliest European travelers to Greece; and Fani-Maria Tsigakou's *The Rediscovery of Greece: Travellers and Painters of the Romantic Era* (London: Thames and Hudson, 1981) is a scholarly study of the way that the Romantic movement colored the thinking of travelers who visited Greece in the nineteenth century.

APPENDIX A   *A Note on the Dates Used in This Work*

Technical information about relative and absolute dating techniques is discussed in many archaeological textbooks. Particularly useful and up-to-date discussions are found in Colin Renfrew and Paul Bahn, *Archaeology: Theories, Methods, and Practice* (New York: Thames and Hudson, 1996). For the reader who just wants the big picture, then William B. Biers's *Art, Artefacts, and Chronology in Classical Archaeology* (London: Routledge, 1992) might just do the trick. If the detailed chronologies for the Greek world given in Biers are not enough, they are also the subject of specialist monographs such as Peter Warren and Vronwy Hankey's *Aegean Bronze Age Chronology* (Bristol, Eng.: Bristol Classical Press, 1989) and Sturt W. Manning's *The Absolute Chronology of the Aegean Early Bronze Age: Archaeology, Radiocarbon, and History* (Sheffield, Eng.: University of Sheffield Press, 1995).

APPENDIX B   *On the Schliemann Trail*

Heinrich Schliemann has been the subject of biographies since his death. Almost all of them, however, suffer from an uncritical use of Schliemann's own numerous autobiographies and only rarely use archival sources such as diaries and letters. As a consequence, most tend to be glowing and appreciative but very uncritical. Typical of this genre are Robert Payne's *The Gold of Troy* (New York: Dorset, 1990) and Emil Ludwig's *Schliemann: The Story of a Gold-Seeker* (Boston: Little, Brown, 1932). With the publication of David Traill's *Schliemann of Troy: Treasure and Deceit* (New York: St. Martin's, 1995) we at last have a full-scale scholarly biography of this fascinating amateur archaeological hero. Some of Traill's conclusions about Schliemann may not be widely accepted (see, e.g., Curtis Runnels, "Review of Schliemann of Troy: Treasure and Deceit," *Journal of Field Archaeology* 24 [1997]: 125–30), but there is no question that Traill's biography will be the standard for some time to come. We recommend that the interested reader sample some of Dr. Schliemann's own writing, rather than relying on the opinions of others; one of his most mature and readable works on archaeology is still widely available in libraries: *Tiryns: The Prehistoric Palace of the Kings of Tiryns* (New York: Charles Scribner's Sons, 1885).

APPENDIX C *Planning an Archaeological Tour of Greece*

Among the many preparations that one can make for a trip to Greece, even an archaeological tour of short duration, a slight acquaintance with the history of the modern Republic of Hellas will be very rewarding. We recommend C. M. Woodhouse's *Modern Greece: A Short History* (London: Faber and Faber, 1992) or Richard Clogg's *A Concise History of Greece* (Cambridge: Cambridge University Press, 1991). An essential traveling companion in Greece for the archaeology student is Robin Barber's *Blue Guide to Greece* (New York: W. W. Norton, 1996). Written by an archaeologist for archaeologists, this handy one-volume guide has directions, plans, illustrations, and excavation histories for all the major sites of every period. Years of experience with this guide have convinced us that it is both reliable and comprehensive.

In this index an "f" after a number indicates a separate reference on the next page, and an "ff" indicates separate references on the next two pages. A continuous discussion over two or more pages is indicated by a span of page numbers. *Passim* is used for a cluster of references in close but not consecutive sequence. Page numbers in italics refer to figure captions.